Don Green

W9-CES-565

BROADCAST
JOURNALISM

BBCY

BROADCAST JOURNALISM

An Introduction to News Writing

Third Edition, Revised

by
MARK W. HALL

COMMUNICATION ARTS BOOKS

HASTINGS HOUSE, PUBLISHERS

Third Edition, Revised, 1986

Library of Congress Cataloging in Publication Data

Hall, Mark W
  Broadcast journalism.

  (Communication arts books)
  Includes index.
  I. Broadcast journalism—Authorship. I. Title.
Library of Congress Catalog Card Number 86-082350
ISBN 0-8038-9287-X

Distributed to the trade by
Kampmann & Company, Inc.,
New York, N.Y.

Printed in the United States of America

10 9 8 7 6 5 4 3 2 1

Contents

5

Preface to the Third Edition

THIS IS NOT JUST ANOTHER BOOK about writing for radio and television. Rather, it is an attempt to combine the specialized technique of writing associated with the world of broadcast journalism with some of the more important approaches developed over the years by experienced newspaper reporters and writers.

As the table of contents indicates, the book covers the basics of radio-television news writing style as well as providing information and guidelines in handling the major types of stories that broadcast journalists might be expected to cover during their careers.

There is no attempt to delve into the mechanical aspects of television; I leave that to someone else. The style proposed in this book can serve efficiently both the radio and television journalist, the latter having only to learn the specific applications of writing for film and television as visual media.

Although the simple listing of the contents does not indicate it, the book uses examples and material that closely reflect what is going on in the "real" world of journalism. Many texts devote much of their time to giving stories that reflect coverage of "safe" events such as beauty contests, city council meetings, church activities and the like. While these are important, it is also essential that the novice journalist be exposed to writing and situations that present the "hot" stories: riots, drug raids, student demonstrations, etc. This is not to say I approve of such happenings; quite to the contrary. I include them since I feel, unpleasant as they may be, a reporter must know how to effectively cover and report them.

The book, while attempting to show good broadcast style, also includes numerous comparative examples to demonstrate clearly how conversational style differs from the style of writing commonly associated with newspapers. It should be noted that the entire book is written in this conversational style to show that it is, in fact, a more easily understood method of writing.

If I were to isolate the major theme of the book, it would be the concept that an electronic newsperson must be a journalist first and a broadcaster second. The book supports the philosophy that the basic skills of reporting must be learned and practiced before one can become a good broadcast journalist. Broadcasting has no room for those who simply want to "rip and read" the news. It is the responsibility of the electronic media to actively recruit and reward those who want to be reporters in the classic sense.

As part of this "news sense," the realization must come that local news is the "bread and butter" of the broadcast journalist. Few of us are fortunate to work for network news departments. For the majority of broadcast journalists, local news, be it for a city as large as New York or as small as Newtown, is the foundation of the daily journalistic effort.

If there is one thing that can be learned from this book, it is the principle that news must be presented in terms of the needs of your local audience. For without it, your news operation will be a dismal failure.

It's been fifteen years since I wrote the first edition of this book. During that time there have been dramatic changes in broadcast technology thanks to advances in micro-circuitry and computer design. However, these new ways of gathering, distributing and packaging news have not changed the role of the writer. It doesn't matter if you use a battered manual typewriter or a sleek word processor; writing is writing. And that's what this book is about. Since my interest is in improving the quality of broadcast news writing, I have spent little time delving into the mysteries of hardware and production techniques. Even though these are valuable components in broadcast news, and good writers need to be aware of the technical capabilities of their news facilities, the main task of a writer is to write.

Chico, California
June 1, 1986

Acknowledgments

WHILE IT IS IMPOSSIBLE to express my true feelings, the author would like to take this opportunity to thank all those that in some way have contributed to the writing of this book: Professors Gordon Greb and James Dunne for first introducing me to the exciting, frustrating and challenging world of broadcast journalism; Professor Rod Gelatt for honing and refining my professional approach to news; Professor Paul Myhre for his stubborn refusal to accept anything less than the best and his honest personal concern—a rare quality; the Leibner Foundation for their limitless financial and moral support; to my parents and my sister for understanding; to Zachary for his steadfast loyalty; and finally, to J.C.D., whose contribution cannot be measured.

1

What Is a
Broadcast Journalist?

YOU ARE ASSUMED TO BE reading this book because you wish to acquire some information and insight that might possibly help you prepare, obtain and hold a job in the world of broadcast journalism. This book will not guarantee any of these things, but it will provide you with the basic tools that will give you a firm foundation for future work in the field. How you use these tools and your future success is entirely predicated on how you approach this specialized field. You will get out of it only what you put into it.

Now then, what is a broadcast reporter? Oddly enough, he or she is a newsperson who works for a radio or television station. If we use the term to mean someone who presents the news, then anyone can fill the slot, from the novice disc-jockey to an advertising salesperson who has a few moments to spare between appointments. However, I do not consider these people journalists; they can only be thought of as ''news readers.''

True broadcast journalists, to indicate their extensive training, are persons specifically trained for reporting the day's events by radio and television. They have received extensive training in the complexities of hard, journalistic reporting combined with a knowledge of radio and television as unique forms of communication.

For electronic journalism to do its job properly, it is essential for the reporters to be good journalists first and newscasters second. Despite the industry's concern for deep, resonant voices and a good camera appearance, it is the person who *knows* news who will make broadcast journalism a valuable addition to the multitude of news voices heard in this country.

This is not to say that voice and camera presence aren't important. But if it were necessary to make a choice between the two, then journalistic ability and knowledge must earn first priority. If I must make some sort of priority order than I would place knowledge first; ability to write coherently and organize a newscast second; and presentation third. Actually, of course, it would be the ideal reporter who had equal ability in all three fields; a worthy goal for any beginner.

But unless you can write and edit a news program it doesn't make much difference how much you know. And unless your delivery is such that you can put your information across to the listener, how much you know and how well you can organize won't serve any purpose. Still, it is all-around knowledge and editing-writing skills that most good news-oriented stations look for first when they are hiring someone to work in their newsrooms.

BACKGROUND KNOWLEDGE

A good journalist must be aware of just about everything that is going on in the world. You must be just as familiar with the inner workings of your local city council as the Security Council of the United Nations. Lack of interest in a particular field, such as sports, is no excuse for ignorance. How can anyone write an intelligent report on a given event with no knowledge of that event and the events that led up to it?

To be a reporter is a 24-hour-a-day job. There is no such thing as a nine-to-five journalist. You must think, eat and breathe news. Being a reporter is probably the most demanding job in the world. Other vocations, even teaching, demand that you become expert in only one narrow field. But a reporter must know about everything. Of course, it is impossible for everyone to be an expert on everything, but you must do your best to at least be aware of what is going on in the world around you.

Now this may sound corny and trite, but unless you are willing to make this type of life-long commitment, you have no right to call yourself a member of the broadcast news profession. Without this kind of dedication, it can practically be guaranteed that you will never rise above the mediocre.

HISTORY OF BROADCAST JOURNALISM

To paraphrase a slogan made popular by the U.S. Census, "We can't know where we're going, unless we know where we've been." For that reason, if only for curiosity's sake, it is essential to take a brief look at the past history—the accomplishments and the failures—of broadcast journalism.

The date of history's first radio broadcast is somewhat obscured by the cloud of academic and professional disagreement over the term *broadcast*.[1] But

---

[1] The problem of honoring the first broadcast is complicated by the various definitions of the word *broadcast*. If we define the term as "simultaneous transmission of information through the air to receivers by electronic means," then why do we call cable television broadcasting? If we accept our definition, what was radio before it became wireless? If it was broadcasting, then we must change our definition to "the transmission of identical sound and/or sight messages simultaneously to multiple

with all this confusion, it is generally accepted by most historians of the subject, that the first radio newscast occurred in 1909 in San Jose, California—some 40 miles south of San Francisco. There, Dr. Charles David Herrold built a tiny experimental radio transmitter and hooked it to an aerial which was strung over downtown streets between the numerous buildings.

Over this spider-web of steel, the good doctor broadcast news and other programs to friends in the area to whom he had provided free crystal sets. As documented by Professor Gordon Greb of San Jose State University's Department of Journalism, Herrold's tiny station (later called KQW) pre-dated the more well-known radio pioneer KDKA of Pittsburgh which went on the air in 1920 and now lays claim to being the world's first radio station.

Regardless of which station was first, the broadcast industry began its meteoric growth during the 1920s; by 1922 there were some 600 stations on the air. Two years later, that number had more than doubled to some 1,400, most of which functioned as promotional sidelines for commercial businesses.

The stations offered music, top names of the entertainment world and other material to amuse the small number of faithful listeners. All of this was financed by the people who owned the stations (at that time there were no commercials) such as General Electric and Westinghouse to further the sale of radio receivers, their prime source of income.

Despite Herrold's fledgling attempts in San Jose to broadcast news, there was practically no attempt made in the early days to do any type of radio reporting on a regular basis. But on rare occasions there were news broadcasts of special events. In August 1920, the *Detroit News* station, 8MK, broadcast returns from the Michigan primary election. Then on November 2 of the same year, station KDKA went on the air and broadcast returns of the Harding-Cox presidential election. Within the next two years groups of stations periodically formed special networks, linked by telephone lines, to provide coverage of special events. Twelve stations formed a network to cover the Republican National Convention in 1924. A year later, 21 stations joined forces to carry President Coolidge's inaugural address from the steps of the Capitol in Washington, D.C.

But the idea of network radio was not yet firmly established. These special networks were created for one time only and ceased to exist after the event. It wasn't until November 15, 1926, that network radio became a permanent part of the broadcasting industry when the National Broadcasting Company (NBC) began serving 25 members of its network. The Columbia Broadcasting System came into existence with 16 stations eight months later in September 1927.

With the rising popularity of radio and its ability to present on-the-spot reports of news events, newspapers began to suffer from loss of advertising reve-

---

listeners in various locations." If this is true, then we can say the first instance of broadcasting took place in the 1860s when Phillip Reis transmitted music via electric wires. There are other numerous incidents of "broadcasting" via telephone lines before the turn of the century. For example, in 1893, Theodore Puskas linked over 700 telephones together to a central broadcasting unit to form the *Telephonic Newspaper* in Budapest.—*JOURNAL OF BROADCASTING,* Summer, 1964.

nue. Potential advertisers soon realized that radio was attracting large numbers of faithful listeners who were potential buyers of their products.

To try and stem this shift of audience and advertising, newspaper owners got together with the three press associations (United Press, Associated Press, and the International News Service) to establish a restrictive news policy against radio. The competition between print and broadcast got so cutthroat at one point that all three services refused to sell any of their news to radio. In retaliation, radio increased its live coverage of single events such as the arrival of Lindbergh in Washington, D.C., in 1927.

Desperate for day-to-day coverage of news events, radio sponsored the formation of new news-gathering organizations to supply news just for radio; companies such as Trans-radio News Service and the Press-Radio News Service enjoyed a few years of financial success during the press service ban.

The press association boycott against radio news was relatively short-lived as pressure from the public continued to mount against the ban. Finally in 1933, the American Newspaper Publisher's Association (ANPA) gave permission to newspaper-owned radio stations to broadcast a limited amount of association news reports—but only if readers were urged to read their local newspaper for further details.

The dam had been broken, and by 1935, UP and INS began selling news on a regular basis to radio stations. AP, which is owned by its members, held out until 1941, but it too supplied news to radio through its separate Press Association service. This was simply a re-written version, in broadcast style, of the news stories carried on the regular AP service.

Today, of course, as we shall see later, both AP and UPI, have radio news divisions which service the broadcasting industry; INS no longer exists, having merged with UP to form UPI (United Press International) some years ago.

During the last half of the 1930s, the networks consolidated their news operations, established permanent programs and created the audience habit of listening to broadcast news coverage.

On December 7, 1941, CBS reporter John Daly interrupted the play-by-play coverage of the Giants-Dodgers football game to tell the country that Japan had attacked Pearl Harbor. That news bulletin marked the beginning of radio's growth into a major news medium—a position it has maintained till this day.

So great was the impact of radio's live, on-the-scene coverage of outstanding events, that 65 per cent of the American radio audience were glued to their radios to hear President Franklin D. Roosevelt ask Congress for a declaration of war against Japan. The following night, the Hooper rating service reported that over 80 per cent of the potential radio audience heard FDR deliver a radio speech on the same subject.[2]

---

[2] The same dependence on electronic journalism was readily apparent during the three days following the assassination of President John F. Kennedy in November 1963. Ratings taken during that period show that 96 per cent of the 59 million homes having television saw some portion of the weekend coverage, and those people who watched television spent an average of 32 hours in front of their sets

The war years spurred radio listening to new heights as people strove to keep up on the latest developments. To meet the demands for up-to-date reports from the battlefields, radio news operations increased their coverage some 30 per cent over pre-war offerings.

World War II provided the motive and the raw material for broadcast news to sharpen its news gathering abilities and techniques. The on-the-spot report, the live interview, the commentary and other current practices all came into being under the heat of battle and were tempered by the demands of the war coverage.

Many well-known names in broadcast journalism gained their first experience with the electronic media during the war years. Journalists such as Howard K. Smith, Robert Trout, Eric Sevareid, George Herman and, of course, Edward R. Murrow who made "This Is London Calling" a household phrase, first gained prominence during the war.

Murrow's contribution to broadcast news is without equal, but unfortunately this is not the proper place to examine his impact on the industry. For that, I suggest you read Fred Friendly's *Due to Circumstances Beyond Our Control* . . . and *Prime Time* by Alexander Kendrick.

The end of the war saw a general lessening of public interest in radio news. The number of hourly bulletins declined and some news programs were cancelled entirely. Other broadcasters dropped news completely and relied totally on wire services for their daily news budget. The practice of "ripping and reading" became commonplace for local radio stations as part-time salesmen, spare announcers and others were pressed into service for five minutes or so every hour on the hour to read the latest news from one of the three press associations. Little effort was put into gathering and reporting local news. But this was all to change; television was rearing its one-eyed head on the electronic horizon.

By the middle of the 1950s, the elaborate network program schedules which had been the mainstay of the majority of American radio stations were pared down to almost nothing except news. This situation still exists today as all four radio networks (ABC, NBC, CBS, and Mutual) serve their affiliates with a steady daily diet of news, commentary and public affairs programming.

Radio stations which had relied heavily on their networks for commercial and programming support suffered heavy financial losses. Many stations were forced out of business, others fought a day-to-day battle against bankruptcy. For a time it looked like radio was dead.

But radio wasn't dead; it came back to life in a newer, even stronger form. Cut off from network programming, local stations were forced to use their own resources to fill the daily schedule.

Independent stations, with their emphasis on local programs, became the new leaders in the radio industry. This focus on the local community opened the way for such programs as recorded music interspersed with information such as

during the three days. In fact, more than 97 million persons watched the High Requiem Mass for the president, and at no point during the three days, even in the early morning hours, were there fewer than seven million viewers.

time, temperature, weather, local road conditions and the like, all geared to local needs. Radio had found its niche—the local market—and used its ability to serve its hometown to build financial success; a success that so far has not been halted.

The backbone of this new type of programming was and still is *news*.

While the early 1950s saw radio struggling to survive, television, after a few financially lean years, broke into its own and began making tremendous strides in programming and production far outstripping what radio had managed to accomplish in the same length of time. This difference can probably be attributed to the simple fact that television learned from radio's mistakes. Television in its early days merely borrowed many of the proven radio programming and production techniques intact from the older medium. Radio, on the other hand, had to painfully experiment and develop on its own; there were no precedents to lead the way.

But television, even with its full color broadcasting, instant replays, communications satellites and all its other expensive hardware, can't compete with radio in four respects.

First, radio is more immediate. Because of the technical complexities involved in a television broadcast, radio is able to begin broadcasting from the scene of an event immediately after the arrival of the reporter. Television, on the other hand, must delay coverage until cameras, microphones, cables and other remote equipment are sent by truck. And then, it may be 30 minutes or so before everything is ready to go.

Second, because of greater schedule flexibility, radio is able to present more news reports during the broadcast day. Television, with its highly structured schedule often holds news reports until its regularly scheduled news programs. Radio, on the other hand, can interrupt its format at a moment's notice for whatever time it takes to present the details on a fast-breaking story.

Third, and probably most important, radio can devote more of its attention to local news. This advantage is more apparent in relatively small markets where the nearest television station might be some 80 miles away while the radio station is operating from within the city limits. Since radio is a much cheaper medium to operate than television, it can afford to limit its audience to a small city. Television, to survive, must control a larger market to provide a big enough audience base to make it worthwhile for advertisers to buy commercial time. Thus television predominately serves a number of communities, which results in a division of its news efforts. Radio can survive by broadcasting to only one area and can then concentrate its energies on extensively covering that one city.

Finally, television's primary contribution to broadcast journalism is its ability to let the audience see as well as hear about some news event. But unless the television camera happens to be on the spot when something breaks (e.g., the explosion of the space shuttle *Challenger*) television can give nothing more than a movie newsreel or a still picture providing a cameraman was there. Radio, however, can convey the impact of an event by words alone which gives it greater flexibility in covering "spot" news.

Technological innovations in the early 1970s saw the introduction of light-weight, portable video recording equipment that increased the ability of television journalists to cover an event quickly. Electronic News Gathering (ENG) involves the use of battery-powered video recorders that permit instant replay of news events without the time-consuming process normally required to develop and edit 16 mm. film.

Many large-market television stations produce live field broadcasts of news events using portable microwave equipment to transmit reports back to the station for direct broadcast. As the cost of such equipment continues to drop, more stations will offer "instant news coverage." However, it will be a long time till ENG equipment will be as fast and easy as a two-way car radio, the staple of radio field reporters.

As broadcast technology improves, the ability of radio to beat television will be threatened. However, the very nature of TV demands more complex and time-consuming hardware, giving the edge, at least for the foreseeable future, to radio.

Television's concern for the visual impact has led to another danger. Because of this insistence upon providing something visual, television news often avoids coverage of the story that doesn't have anything visual, and too often makes editorial decisions based on the availability of pictures, rather than true news value.

It is hard to deny that the majority of people in America get a major share of their daily news from television. It is also hard to dispute the hard reality that most Americans turn to television for coverage of planned events such as the lunar flights, political conventions and sports.

When we look at the total broadcast journalism picture, radio makes a better showing. The importance of the medium to American listeners is shown in research data. A 1985 study, Radio's All Dimension Audience Research, indicated that 182 million listen to radio each week; that's more than 96 per cent of everyone over 12 years of age. A CBS-commissioned survey in 1983 showed that radio was the primary source of morning news for 56 per cent of those questioned while television was named by only 21 per cent.

People turn to television for extensive coverage of news events, but an overwhelming percentage of the potential audience turn on their radio to find out the first reports of a news story. A 1968 survey showed that some 56.6 per cent of those questioned learned from radio that Senator Robert Kennedy had been shot, while only 20.2 per cent heard about the shooting from television.

Since the assassination of President Kennedy occurred on November 22, 1963, at noon, people reported first hearing of the event from others and then turning to radio and then to television to follow the subsequent events.

Similar audience research has reported that just under 80 per cent of the adult audience rely on radio for weather news, the remaining 20 per cent divided between television and newspapers.

This heavy reliance on radio for news and information was not an overnight phenomenon. A *Fortune* magazine survey in 1939 showed that about 63 per cent of the sample got their news from newspapers. Six years later, a survey by the National Opinion Research Center said 61 per cent got their news first from radio, a shift perhaps prompted by the urgency of World War II. The most recent research indicates a definite pattern in the reliance on radio for news; especially in the morning when radio news is most abundant.

While proponents of radio are busy applauding the audience's reliance on their medium, television supporters are quick to wave their research results in defense. According to the 1974 Roper survey just over two-thirds of those asked said television was their source for ". . . most of the news about what's going on in the world." This represents a 14 point rise from the 51 per cent figure reported in a 1959 survey. Radio scored a mere 21 per cent; 13 points lower than a 1959 showing of 34 per cent.

Unfortunately, these results are not surprising considering the general slow-down in radio-news operations. Except for major markets where millions of dollars are spent to capture the elusive, largely male, drive-time audience with a heavy dose of news, weather and sports, radio news is in a sad state of decline. Many small-market stations have succumbed to the lure of automation and have sacrificed news departments to offer pre-packaged programming.

Despite the pessimistic state of radio news broadcasting, it still remains the number-one source for information about fast-breaking news events. Radio, with its ability to communicate immediately, will probably continue to be the medium most often used first; the "early-warning system" of our media network.

2

Writing for Radio and Television News

IT IS ASSUMED THAT you will have already received sufficient exposure to the basic techniques of journalism and news gathering. Therefore, I shall deal with the peculiar aspects of radio and television news-writing as a technique differing in style, approach and rationale from news-writing designed for the print media. Notice, I do not include basic journalistic concepts in these differences. The techniques of good reporting apply equally to both print and broadcast news; it is only the technique of writing that differs.[1]

Everything that you have learned about the gathering of news, the analyzing and selecting of newsworthy features; the treatment of straight news; the importance of the lead; and the general principles of attribution, identification, and objectivity are a vital part of broadcast journalism. All of these are basic skills, applicable to all news media: radio, television, newspapers or magazines. The similarities between the various media far outweigh the differences in style and approach which the characteristics of the particular medium dictate.

CONVERSATIONAL STYLE

The basic difference between print and broadcast journalism is that the former is designed for the eye, while the latter is produced for the ear. This gives newspaper reporters a slight advantage when they sit down at the typewriter, fingers poised to bang out a story. They don't have to be particularly concerned about the complexity of their sentences. Even if a sentence includes four or five dependent clauses, the reader can simply read the phrase over and over again until it makes sense.

[1] See Appendix A for complete style guide.

The broadcast writer does not have this luxury. A story is read and *heard* only once. If the listener is confused by a particularly complex sentence, he is out of luck. He can't ask the newscaster to repeat some confusing point. The listener has to be able to understand the story the first time; there's no chance to repeat.

Since broadcast journalism is designed for the ear, it is important you write what has been called "hear" copy rather than "see" copy which is the hallmark of newspapers.

Newscasts are written in conversational style, the informal manner in which a person ordinarily speaks. Sentences are kept relatively short and straight to the point. The simple declarative statement is preferred:

NEWSPAPER: Her face flushed wth heat, she stumbled up the weather-beaten steps, flung open the door, and stepped inside.

BROADCASTING: Her face was flushed with heat as she stumbled up the weather-beaten steps. She flung open the door and stepped inside.

Complex sentence structure, little-known words and other literary techniques should be used carefully because they tend to be misunderstood when heard even though they make sense when they are read. Consider the following typical newspaper lead. Read it aloud to a friend and see if she can tell you what it says:

Speeding to the bedside of his dying wife, Walter Smith, a Bell Telephone company repairman, was seriously injured today when he was thrown through the windshield of his truck after it collided with another car driven by Melvin Potts, 33, of South Danbury, New York, who, police say, was driving with a suspended driver's license.

In general the following are some of the major differences between print and broadcast style:

1. The inverted sentence structure used in newspaper writing is avoided in broadcast news.

NEWSPAPER: There is no danger from further flooding in the area, according to Walter Thompson, director of the North Coast Flood Control District.

BROADCASTING: The director of the North Coast Flood Control District, Walter Thompson, says there is no danger from further flooding in the area.

2. Sentences are kept short in radio-TV writing, almost to the point of oversimplification:

NEWSPAPER: The present tax base of three dollars, which is a 30 per cent increase over last year's rate, but down from five years ago, will be increased another two per cent as of June 1 if tomorrow's tax over-ride election is successful.

BROADCASTING: If tomorrow's tax over-ride election is successful the present tax base of three dollars will be increased two per cent June first. The present rate is 30 per cent higher than last year, but is still lower than it was five years ago.

3. Subjects and verbs are kept close together whenever possible.

NEWSPAPER: Cosa Nostra boss Nick "the Spaniard" Gomez, who has often refused to testify before the U.S. Senate Committee on Crime and, who is well known for his dealings in labor rackets, illegal gambling and drug smuggling, was arrested today for refusal to pay last year's federal income tax.

BROADCASTING: Cosa Nostra boss Nick "the Spaniard" Gomez has been arrested for refusing to pay last year's federal income tax. He is well known for his dealings in labor rackets, illegal gambling, and drug smuggling. Gomez has often refused to testify before the U.S. Senate Committee on Crime.

4. Identification of subjects such as age, job title and the like come before the name in radio-TV writing, rather than after.

NEWSPAPER: William Jones, 43, chief supervisor for District Number Five of the Narcotics Control Bureau said. . . .

BROADCASTING: The chief supervisor for District Five of the Narcotics Control Bureau, 43-year old William Jones said. . . .

5. In broadcast writing it is permissible, and often required for clarity, that incomplete sentences be written.

NEWSPAPER: The black acrid smoke billowed from the uncontrolled oil rig fire leaving a swath of choking lungs and tear-filled eyes.

BROADCASTING: Choking lungs . . . tear-filled eyes . . . those were the results of the black acrid smoke which billowed from the uncontrolled oil rig fire.

There is one danger in writing in the conversational style: verbosity. Once you are aware of this pitfall, the way you would *tell* the story to an interested questioner is a good guide as to how you should *write* the story for your listeners.

Careful rereading *out loud* will catch errors and point out sloppy writing. This emphasis on "hear" copy has been carried to its ultimate by the news service of the British Broadcasting Corporation (BBC) which insists that its news writers dictate their stories to a secretary who types the final script. This may seem a bit extravagant to us, but it does force the writer to think in terms of "hear" copy rather than "see" copy.

The reporter who wrote the following lead for a late night newscast obviously didn't reread the copy to see if it made sense:

>After fatally shooting himself, 42-year old Robert Hall was taken to the county emergency hospital where he later died.

How can someone who is "fatally" shot die later? The word *fatally* means dead.

REWRITING WIRE COPY TO LOCALIZE

Relying on "rip and read" wire copy which is used *verbatim* from the wire service machine is no guarantee of good "hear" copy. In fact, it should be a cardinal rule in any news operation that copy from the press associations should never be read as is. It should be considered nothing more than the raw material from which the reporter tailors a story to fit local needs and interests.

If deadlines and small newsroom staffs make it impossible to rewrite all of the wire copy, an attempt must be made to at least pre-read the material before going on the air to make sure it makes sense when read out loud.

This warning is imperative for a number of reasons.

First, wire service material is written for newspaper deadlines and, as United Press International likes to boast, there's always a deadline somewhere in the world. This concern for deadlines means the wire services must be constantly up-dating stories during the day. They are not concerned with making sure the stories are in some sort of logical sequence: that one item about the president will not duplicate an earlier story; that one story on drugs will be five stories away from a similar report from another part of the state; or that the part of the story of most importance to your audience won't be in the last paragraph rather than in the lead.

Second, the broadcast service of both press associations is often treated like stepchild. Unfortunately, both organizations reportedly put their most inexperienced writers on the radio news desk. Few of these writers get out in the field to prepare first hand reports. Radio news, in many instances, is nothing more than standard newspaper wire copy shunted over the radio desk for rewriting for distribution to radio and TV stations. The result is often disappointing. Often unfamiliar with the nuances of "good writing," the writers manning the rewrite desks many times prepare their copy with one hand on a style book and the other pounding the typewriter. This formula approach produces writing that is often stereotyped and stodgy; writing that fairly begs for local reworking.

Finally, wire associations are preparing copy for clients all over the world. They must emphasize the aspect of the story that has the most general interest. It would be impossible for them to "localize" each story to fit your area. Therefore, it is left to the local station to take the wire copy, and rewrite it to find the local angle that will tell listeners what is important about the event; why they should pay attention to the details of the devaluation of the *franc,* for example.

This search for the local angle is probably the most important reason for rewriting. The needs of an audience differ from area to area, from station to station. And if a newscast is to succeed in presenting information about the world, it must put it in terms *its* audience will understand and see as relevant. There is hardly a report, regardless of geographic origination, that cannot be localized and brought into perspective.

"Ripping and reading" can lead you to miss important local stories. Say your Mission Hills radio station receives the following from UPI. "Ripping and reading" without rewriting would bury the one local name so far down in the story it would be missed by almost everyone:

(Casualties)

(Washington)—The Defense Department has announced the names of 25 servicemen killed in a crash of a C-135 transport plane near Hartford, Maine. They included the following men from California and Nevada:

Master Sergeant John A-B Dill Junior, husband of Mrs. Bette Dill of Corte Madera.

Army Captain Robert Mance, husband of Mrs. Nancy Mance of Sacramento.

Army Sergeant John Wille, son of Mr. and Mrs. Wille of West Covina.

Army Private First Class Douglas Weston, son of Mr. and Mrs. Stephen Weston of Hacienda Heights.

Army Specialist Four William Gold, son of Mr. and Mrs. Kenneth Gold of Mission Hills.

VR537PPD5/18 [Names have been changed.]

Rewriting for your local audience would see the final casuality moved up and made the lead:

A Mission Hills man, Army Specialist Four William Gold, son of Mr. and Mrs. Kenneth Gold, is included in the latest list of servicemen killed in a plane crash. . . .

Not only does rewriting give you a locally-oriented story, but it does a number of other things that will help a news operation out-perform its competition:[2] (1) It gives your station a different "sound." Since many stations subscribe to the same service, all reports sound alike. Rewriting gives you a new version. (2) It gives you the opportunity to correct mistakes the wire service may have made. (3) It allows you to up-date stories, placing the most recent development in the lead. And, (4) rewriting gives you the chance to consolidate various items under one comprehensive lead.

REWRITING TO UPDATE

There is another important reason to rewrite the news—boredom. Radio news, unlike a newspaper, is presented a number of times throughout the day. Often, a radio station will feature news twice an hour; that's 48 reports in a 24 hour day. While some of the items in each newscast will be fresh, much will be

[2] See Chapter 5, Pages 121–122 for further examples of localizing wire copy reports of disasters.

carry-overs from earlier reports. Since the majority of your audience tends to listen to the same station all day, if you do not make an attempt to freshen old copy for each newscast you will lose many of them out of sheer boredom.

From a strictly commercial viewpoint consider the following situation. There are two radio stations in a small city. Both have hourly newscasts throughout the day. Station X relies on the wire services for its reports, giving little attention to the problem of repetition. Station Y, on the other hand, goes out of its way to freshen its copy each hour, giving new developments top priority. Which one do you think will be the most successful in the long run?

Rewriting your stories accomplishes two goals in addition to the ones mentioned previously: it presents new angles and developments; and it makes the news sound fresher, giving your station a "different" sound than its competition.

There are three basic rules which should be emblazoned in fiery letters on every newsroom wall:

1. Rewrite every story of the same event emphasizing the newest angle or development.
2. Rewrite every item of a "running" (continuing) story making sure that as a minimum you rewrite the lead.
3. Rewrite all wire copy in terms of local news and audience needs when possible.

It takes a skilled writer to rewrite a news item without distorting the essence of the story. The writer must be able to take a story and dig up an angle or a new twist that makes the story different than the one aired the previous hour.

Most of the news in any newscast is related in some way to other news. It usually takes more than one report to tell the full story. After the first account has been broadcast, there are usually new developments which must be reported. And it is this ability to "up-date" which separates the good writer from the hack.

The skill to pick aspects of a news story which must be investigated further is a valuable asset to a reporter and writer. This "follow-up" procedure is the major reason why all radio news operations should subscribe to the local newspapers, monitor the competition and keep abreast of developments in the national media.

The day of the exclusive story, the "scoop," is gone. Most major news sources these days are conscious of their relationships with the news media and go out of their way to inform all of them of the latest development. Transportation and communication facilities have become so efficient that it is now almost impossible to keep a story "under wraps."

Thus it is perfectly acceptable for one medium to use another for an idea for a story. I am not suggesting *verbatim* copying from other media; that is not only unethical but illegal. But I urge you to use the other media as "idea sparkers." Read the local newspaper, listen to your competition, and if they have a story you do not have, then go out and develop your own report on the same event using their story as a primary source for names, leads, etc.

When you begin to rewrite an earlier story there are a number of points that you should emphasize in your new version:

1. New information not available when the first story was presented
2. Causes and motives not included in the first report
3. Results and consequences of the first story
4. Opinions about the event
5. The significance of the event in light of local developments

Latest developments surrounding the event should always be emphasized in the lead. And since radio specializes in what is happening "now," the best lead in a rewrite is a present or future tense slant.

For example your nine o'clock newscast featured a story that reported the arrest of three students for staging a sit-in to protest the firing of five professors. The first version might highlight the fact that they were just arrested; your second story, aired at noon of the same day, might lead with the fact that they are still in jail; while your third might feature a new development.

NINE O'CLOCK: Three college students have been arrested by local police for staging a sit-in to protest the firing of five professors. There was no violence reported on the campus.

NOON REPORT: Those three college students arrested for staging a sit-in are still in jail at this hour. They have not yet been formally charged by police who say they were breaking the law by blocking the entrance to the college's administration building. The sit-in was staged to protest the firing of five professors.

SIX O'CLOCK: Formal charges of disturbing the peace have been filed against those three college students arrested this morning for staging a sit-in to protest the firing of five professors. Trial date has not been set.

Finally at 11 o'clock, the same story might feature another angle:

The trial date for those three students arrested today for staging a sit-in has not yet been set. Earlier today the trio . . . who were protesting the firing of five faculty members . . . were formally charged with disturbing the peace.

Notice while each of the follow-up stories features a new development, a "tie-back," was prominently included. Never should the writer assume that the audience has heard the previous reports. Just as the movie serials of Saturday afternoon fame prefaced each chapter with a brief resume of previous developments, so should your up-dates.[3]

This "tie-back" is usually inserted in the lead in the form of a phrase or dependent clause, but any grammatical device can be used. Sometimes the tie-back may be delayed until the second paragraph.

But whatever technique you use, it is essential that your stories emphasize

[3] See Appendix C for further examples of up-dating.

the latest developments. Consider the following examples and notice how the second version emphasizes the "now" aspect:

> POOR: The City Council last night voted to install new traffic signals in the downtown area to ease the flow of traffic.
> BETTER: Traffic flow in the downtown district will hopefully be smoother in the future as the City Council last night voted to install new traffic signals in the area.

Another angle to look for while rewriting is the cause or motive for the event:

> ORIGINAL STORY: Five persons are dead this evening following a five alarm blaze which leveled a three story apartment building in downtown Redding. The fire started on the first floor and quickly spread through the wooden frame building. . . .
> REWRITE: Arson investigators are now saying this morning's blaze which gutted a downtown Redding apartment building was deliberately set. Fire Chief Ronald Woods says, and we quote, "That fire was not accidental." . . .

A new development in a running story provides the lead in this example: [4]

> ORIGINAL STORY: A local man who was trapped for a week in the crumpled wreckage of his small private plane was found this morning by an Air Force rescue team. 42-year-old Robert Kelly was taken to the county hospital where he is listed in critical condition. . . .
> REWRITE: That local man who survived for a week while trapped in the wreckage of his small private plane before being rescued this morning has died. 42-year-old Robert Kelly died less than an hour ago from severe internal injuries. . . .

If there is no "real" new development in a story, it is possible to up-date the report by seeking opinions on the event from sources who might be affected:

> ORIGINAL STORY: Five New York City office buildings were ripped apart this morning by powerful explosives. At least ten people are feared dead. Police are not sure of the final death count since the rubble is still too hot to allow a search for survivors. A note delivered to a New Jersey radio station claimed credit for setting the explosions. The hand-written message was signed by a group calling itself the Liberation Force for a Free America. . . .
> REWRITE: New York City police continue their search for those responsible for this morning's bombing of five downtown office buildings. A note from a group calling itself the Liberation Force for a Free America claimed responsibility for the multiple bombing that left at least ten dead. Police ex-

---

[4] See Chapter 3, Page 55 for further examples of up-dating.

perts are working to determine the source of the note which was delivered to a New Jersey radio station shortly after the bombs exploded. . . .

Occasionally an important news story breaks too fast to permit investigation of its feature possibilities. If you find yourself stuck with little new facts or developments, you might simply retell the story in a different feature approach:

ORIGINAL STORY: A freak combination of events has lead to the arrest of a local man on charges of fraud. It seems 23-year old David Rivers was sitting in a local tavern when he was approached by a stranger who. . . .
REWRITE: The old cliche ". . . never trust a stranger . . ." proved true today and led to the arrest of a local man on charges of fraud. . . .

We have already discussed the importance of localizing news to your particular market. This technique can also be applied to rewriting from other media. For example, *Time* magazine might feature a story documenting the problems of air pollution in New York City. An alert reporter reading the article might ask if the local area has the same problem, and if not, why not. An investigation might lead to the following feature piece:

While New York City, Washington D.C., and Los Angeles might have their problems with smog . . . our area is relatively free of dirty air. To find out why, we checked with. . . .

Very often a hard news story may jog the memory of one of the older reporters in the newsroom and lead to an historical feature piece which draws parallels between the present and the past and relates anecdotes brought to mind by the present event.

For example, the manager of your local airport announces that in two weeks there will be daily jet service to your area. Of course this announcement is news and you would cover it, probably including statements from airport, airline, and city officials about the reasons for and impact of the new service. But you might also want to rewrite the story into a feature which highlights the historic development of air service to your city or area:

Jet planes will begin landing at Civic Airport next week. This does not sound like an historic event to those of us familiar with modern air travel. But to some of the older residents of our city who can remember when the airport was nothing more than the "back 40" whose sole population was a couple of red heifers and some scraggly sheep . . . we have come a long way in 15 years. . . .

The reporter assigned to rewrite a news story must, of course, obey all the rules of good news writing. This means, among other things, that the story lead must play up the feature of the item.

This is not as easy as it sounds since if the original was well written, the obvious feature angle will have already been exploited. It is the poorly written story that is the easiest to rewrite.

With no new facts at his disposal, the reporter faced with a rewrite job must ask a number of questions before starting:

1. In the case of stories appearing in media outside the local area, is there a local angle that can be played up?

2. Are there any other news stories that can be combined with the story to give an overall view of the event?

3. Failing the availability of other similar stories, can a comprehensive lead be written which will tie this report to others?

4. Did the original play up the real feature or is it buried some place in the article?

5. Is the original written in such a manner that it will be of interest to *our* audience?

Local Angle

As discussed in the previous section, the reporter who reads newspapers from other cities will occasionally run across an item that may be rewritten for local consumption:

> ORIGINAL: A nationwide contribution drive for the Heart Fund was officially kicked off here [Chicago] today. Goal of the campaign has been set at 50 million dollars for the midwest region. Dr. Ronald Faster of Chicago was elected campaign chairman. Other officers include: William Douglas of Cincinnati, who will be area coordinator . . . Stephen Harris of St. Louis, chairman, and Helen McDonald of Columbia, Missouri, publicity director. . . .
>
> REWRITE: (For St. Louis station) A local man . . . Stephen Harris . . . will be the state chairman of this year's Heart Fund charity drive. He was elected during kick-off ceremonies held in Chicago recently. Announced goal for the nationwide campaign is set at 50 million dollars. Another Missourian . . . Helen McDonald of Columbia . . . was elected publicity chairman. . . .

Combining Stories:

The following example shows how one writer combined two separate items into a single story:

> ORIGINAL: [from UPI] The San Francisco Giants announced today they have traded utility outfield Jesus Ramos to the Chicago White Sox for three future draft choices and an undisclosed amount of cash. . . . The San Francisco 49'ers say they are trading quarterback Billy Hargis to the Pittsburgh Steelers for a badly needed interior lineman. . . .
>
> REWRITE: Trades are the big news today from the front offices of San Francisco's baseball and football teams. . . . The Giants have traded utility outfielder Jesus Ramos to the Chicago White Sox . . . and the 49'ers got a

badly needed interior lineman for quarterback Billy Hargis who went to the Pittsburgh Steelers. . . .

Comprehensive Lead:

Often the writer's knowledge about recent events will help to prepare a lead that ties the single story to other events which have recently been in the news:

ORIGINAL: A local high school student . . . 17-year-old Jane Miner . . . has been selected as the winner of the national "Girl of the Year" award. The straight-"A" student . . . who has also received prominent notice for her performance on the tennis team . . . will go to Washington, D.C., to receive her award from the president. . . .

REWRITE: For the second time in as many years, a local high school student has been chosen for the national "Girl of the Year" award. 17-year-old Jane Miner will go to Washington D.C. to receive her award from the president. . . .

Buried Feature:

If the writer of the original story has missed the feature, the task of rewriting the item is quite simple:

ORIGINAL: The question of closing First Street was again the major bone of contention at last night's City Council meeting. Councilman John Older presented a list of arguments against closing the street, insisting that to do so would cost the city more than 100-thousand dollars in the near future. Speaking in favor of the closing was Councilman Walter Johnson who pointed out that closing the street would improve the flow of traffic in the downtown area. The Council voted five to two to submit the question to the voters in a special election set for March 25.

REWRITE: The City Council has given voters the chance to decide whether to close First Street. Last night the council voted five to two to put the issue before the public in a special election set for March 25.

Local Interests:

Quite often a national story is written in terms of national interests. As previously pointed out, without additional facts, it is still possible to rewrite the story to spark the interest of local listeners:

ORIGINAL: The Federal Budget Bureau disclosed today that the national cost of living level has increased five percent in the past year. . . .

REWRITE: It's costing local residents five cents more this year to buy what cost a dollar a year ago. So says the Federal Budget Bureau which disclosed today its cost of living index rose by five per cent over the past twelve months.

VERB TENSES

Many years ago when newspapers travelled in pony express pouches or dusty railroad mail cars, it was common for weeks to pass before details of an event reached San Francisco from New York City. This delay forced newspapers to emphasize the time element by using a dateline in the lead (LONDON, Monday, Dec. 8 UPI) to tell the reader when the story was dispatched so he would know how old the report might be. Transportation and communication facilities have improved since the days of the clipper ship but the dateline tradition continues in most newspaper stories prepared by the various press services.

Both UPI and AP use the name of the day in their stories. This is in keeping with the special requirements of print journalism which, at best, is several hours old when it finally hits your front porch. Newspapers cannot, and never will be in their present form, a medium of immediacy. There is no possible way for them to match the swiftness of their electronic brethren; by their very nature they are not expected to.

Broadcast journalists, however, are not shackled to the time-consuming process of publishing a newspaper; their news is "right now." Therefore, it is usually not necessary to include the name of the day in each story, rather the word *today* suffices; and for that matter, the words *yesterday* and *tomorrow*.

For example, a story appearing in the Tuesday morning edition of the local newspaper might carry the following item:

The City Council, at the end of Monday night's meeting, *expressed* unanimous support for the proposal submitted by Ecology Action, Incorporated which *called* for a city ordinance to forbid open burning during the summer months, a period of high air pollution.

The broadcaster might handle the same item in this manner the following morning:

The City Council *has given* its unanimous support to a proposal from Ecology Action, Incorporated which *is calling* for a city ordinance to ban open burning during the summer months . . . a period of high air pollution. The council took the action at the end of last night's meeting.

You will notice that even though the council's action took place in the past (Monday night), the broadcast version de-emphasizes this aspect of the story and instead brings it more into the present by the use of the present perfect verb *has given*. The exact time of the action is delayed until the end of the item.

A comparison of the other verbs in the sentence shows another standard broadcasting technique which is different from newspaper style—the use of present tense verbs instead of past tense.

As I have pointed out, the print media must use the past tense for a majority of stories because they are dated. But since broadcast reports are not dated to that extent what reads correctly sounds silly when spoken. For example, consider the statement: "The president *said* he *thought* the vice president *was doing* a good job." Read aloud, it makes one wonder if the president still thinks so. Of course he does, so say so: "The president *says* he *thinks* the vice president *is doing* a good job." If somebody thinks about something in the past, you can assume, unless you know to the contrary, that he still thinks so now.

Here's a few examples of how to make news more immediate for broadcasting:

A newspaper press wire carries a story that the president has left Washington for his weekend retreat. The newspaper has to write the story in the past tense because of the reason already discussed.

But radio and television are so much faster, they can report the news while the president is still enroute: "The president *is* flying to his weekend retreat . . ."

Or we might use the present perfect and say: "The president **has left** Washington for his weekend retreat."

Or we might look to the future: "The president **will arrive** at his weekend retreat within the hour, after leaving Washington earlier this morning."

You can emphasize immediacy by verb tense and by connecting it to some time reference such as:

> Moments ago. . . .
> Just before news time. . . .
> At this hour. . . .
> At this very moment. . . .

But overuse of these phrases should be avoided or they will become commonplace and lose their impact.

Another caution: occasionally, the text of a speech will be released for use before it is actually delivered. Think of how silly you will sound if you quote a speaker as having *said* something based on his printed speech, when it later turns out that during that speech he made some revisions and didn't say it. This situation clearly calls for a guarded use of the future tense: "The senator . . . in a speech to be delivered tonight . . . will call for increased support of educational programs." Or, "In a prepared speech scheduled for tonight, the senator will accuse. . . ." To protect yourself against changes in the speaker's prepared text, you should make it perfectly clear in your story that your information comes from an advance copy of the speech.

Sometimes it is necessary to mix past and present tenses to keep from confusing the logical order of the story, parts of which may appropriately be completed in the past while others are handled as on-going items.

For example, in the following three versions of the same story, notice that the past tense version has the least immediacy, the present tense the most, and the mixture of the two keeps the listener clear as to what action is continuing and which is completed:

PAST TENSE: The president *announced* today he will speak to Congress next Wednesday on the current threat posed by international terrorism. He *said* he will detail his plans to deal with the crisis.

PRESENT TENSE: The president *is* preparing his plans to deal with international terrorism, which he will deliver during an address to Congress next Wednesday. In an announcement released this morning, the president *says* he will detail his plans to deal with the crisis.

MIXTURE OF TENSES: The president *is* preparing a speech on the current problem of international terrorism, which he will deliver during an address to Congress next Wednesday. The president *said* today he will outline his plans to deal with the crisis.

The last version emphasizes immediacy in the lead, then deals with the announcement in the past tense because the action is completed in the past.

A word of warning—don't get carried away with this desire to put everything into the present tense. Don't use present tense verbs for events that logically belong in the past. In some stories, accuracy and clarity call for the use of past tense verbs. It is illogical and confusing to use present tense verbs to describe a past situation which is over and has no possible chance of continuing into the present.

It is impossible to give a list of situations that demand the use of the past tense. Each writer must use common sense to determine when past, not present tense, is called for; reading copy out loud will go a long way towards revealing these problem areas.

Consider the following item, a report of a fire which killed 12 and injured three, in terms of using past or present tense verbs.

A five-alarm fire, which *swept* through a downtown apartment building last night, *has killed* 12 persons and injured three others.

It would be ridiculous to use the present tense to report this story:

A five-alarm fire, which *is sweeping* through a downtown apartment building last night *is killing* 12 persons and injuring three others.

However, it is possible to make the story have more of a sense of immediacy by using the gerund form of the verb. For example:

A fire-alarm fire swept through a downtown apartment building last night *killing* 12 persons and injuring three others.

Not only is the story more immediate, but I have saved one word, "which," and made the sentence flow more easily.

NAMES OF PERSONS

"Names make news," is a trite but true axiom for all forms of news—be it newspapers, magazines or radio-television.[5]

Everyone is interested in what other people are doing. And if that other person is known to the reader or listener, that interest is heightened. Next time you read your daily newspaper, notice how your eye and attention are captured by headlines that display the name of someone, something, or someplace that you are familiar with. The same is true for radio and television, only the rules covering the use of names are a bit different.

In newspaper copy it is the name in the lead that grabs the reader's attention. But in broadcast news, if you lead with the name, the listener isn't "ready" for it and he will probably not hear the name and will then spend the rest of the story wondering who you are talking about.

Therefore, it is essential to "cue" the listener that a name is coming up in the story. You do this by simply using a descriptive phrase before the name. Consider the following newspaper item about a narcotics raid that featured the arrest of the mayor's son:

Thomas Joseph, 23, the son of South Rafael Mayor Robert Joseph was among 25 college students arrested last night by local police in a series of raids on numerous student living centers. Joseph was arraigned this morning before Judge Hiram Gubbins in Butte County Superior Court, and charged with three counts of marijuana possession. The other students. . . .

There is nothing wrong with this item, for newspapers that is; but, if you were to read it on a radio newscast most listeners would miss the name of the mayor's son since they weren't "prepared" to hear it. This problem can be solved by rewriting the item which also includes a shifting of events to "update" the story:

The son of South Rafael Mayor Robert Joseph has been charged with three counts of marijuana possession. 23-year-old Thomas Joseph appeared before Butte County Superior Court Judge Hiram Gubbins for arraignment after he was arrested last night during a series of raids on numerous local student living centers. Joseph was among 25 students arrested on various narcotics violations . . . none of the others have yet been formally charged.

Notice I have delayed the name until after the identifying phrase, and then repeated the name a second time for good measure.

The general rule, then, is to delay most names (of people, places, and things) until the second or third sentence. Of course, if the name is widely known and is an attention-getting device on its own, then it is permissible for it to begin the story. For example, it would be foolish to delay the name in the following item; doing so might border on the absurd:

> The president is scheduled to talk to the astronauts late this evening to offer his personal congratulations for a successful moon landing.

Rewriting to delay the name might give you this:

> The president of the United States is scheduled to talk to the astronauts late this evening. He will offer his personal congratulations for a successful moon landing.

But if you do lead with a name, make sure it is well known to all your listeners. Those who know the name won't be insulted by the delay of that name, but those who don't will be upset by missing it.

Sometimes, it is better not to use names at all, especially when the story includes no local persons. For example, a report of an airplane crash in Chicago which kills 135 passengers is important, but the names are meaningless to your non-Chicago listeners. Thus you should just feature the number of passengers rather than the names. Of course, you should scan the passenger list to make sure no local people are involved. If they are, then their names would be prominently featured.

The following story on a massive train wreck in the Midwest moves on the wire services. Down near the bottom of the story, the name of a local person is listed as being among the dead. An alert writer would move the local angle into the lead, and write the following:

> A local businessman is listed as being one of the 85 victims of today's massive train wreck in Illinois. 35-year-old Gregory Henderson died in the explosion that followed the two train collision.

You will note that even in this story, the name has been delayed until the late part of the lead sentence.

Newspapers, in their desire to be accurate and keep true historical records give the full names and addresses of all persons involved in the news, especially local stories. Radio and television, on the other hand, handle full names and title a bit differently. Use them for what they are, for properly identifying people. Try to avoid getting bogged down in a maze of confusing titles and middle initials. Radio-television news omits middle initials and unless they have become widely known as an integral part of the name, such as Howard K. Smith, John L. Lewis, J. Paul Getty, etc. The same rule applies to full names; they would only be used when the person is normally identified in that manner: Henry Cabot Lodge, George Bernard Shaw, William Jennings Bryan, etc.

By and large, however, the use of the middle initial or the full name on the air simply clutters up the copy and confuses the listener, and is not at all necessary for proper identification. Herbert C. Hoover, Richard Milhouse Nixon, Lyndon Baines Johnson all add nothing and merely require the listener to pay more attention to detail.

TITLES

In conversation, as well as broadcast writing, use titles *before* names unless the structure becomes awkward (another reason to read copy out loud as you write).[6] Putting the title first makes the copy flow instead of breaking it up with a lot of unnecessary commas:

> NEWSPAPER: Robert M. Jones, regional director for the Federal Narcotics Bureau, said today. . . .
> BROADCASTING: The regional director for the Federal Narcotics Bureau Robert Jones said today. . . .
> NEWSPAPER: Senator Allen Cranston (Dem.Cal.)
> BROADCASTING: California Democratic Senator Allen Cranston
> NEWSPAPER: Frank R. Blythe, chairman, General Motors Buick Division, said today in Detroit. . . .
> BROADCASTING: The chairman of General Motor's Buick Division Frank Blythe said today in Detroit. . . .

Note how the restructuring of the sentence eliminates the commas which makes the copy flow and sound smoother to the ear of the listener. But remember that sometimes putting the title first makes the sentence sound jarring. If that happens, put the name first. The cardinal goal is clarity, not blind faith in a style book.

As far as repeating the titles in a second reference is concerned (such as Captain Smith), broadcast writers usually don't with few exceptions.

Generally, use a title for the president of the United States every time his name is used. Call him President Reagan or Mr. Reagan. This editorial privilege is normally not accorded to anyone else in public office except where local practice dictates otherwise.

Another exception is in the naming of clergymen. It's common practice to use a title for members of the clergy each time their name is used:

> *Example 1:* A Chicago soldier, Army Captain Louis Haynes has been formally charged with desertion of duty . . . Haynes is being held at Fort Monmouth, New Jersey. . . .
> *Example 2:* San Francisco surgeon Dr. Susan Taylor has been elected president of the American Medical Association during the group's annual meeting in Pittsburgh. Taylor is a member of the University Board of Surgery.
> *Exception 1:* President Reagan today lashed out at his political opponents, calling them politically naive. Mr. Reagan made the remarks during a breakfast at the White House. The president was reacting to. . . .
> *Exception 2:* A Birmingham, Alabama minister the Reverend Mr. William Brace has pleaded guilty to disorderly conduct after he was arrested for leading a recent voter registration march through the city's downtown area. . . . The Reverend Mr. Brace was fined 100 dollars. . . .

[6] See Appendix A, Style Guide, page 117.

Often it is better to substitute titles for names. This is particularly true when the name is obscure, hard to pronounce, or not needed for understanding the story, and especially when the news concerns the office rather than the office holder. Common sense will tell you that it is almost meaningless to bother your listeners with the names of government officials from foreign countries when they probably won't remember the name anyway. The same thing can be said for the names of minor government officials in our own country.

So, while newspaper editors insist on printing the full name and title of all officials, radio and television can, and do, leave out obscure names:

> NEWSPAPER: Julio Jimenez, the conservation director of Mexico, said smog is threatening Mexico City. . . .
> BROADCASTING: Mexico's director of conservation says smog is threatening Mexico City. . . .
> NEWSPAPER: Sir Malcolm Smythe, under-secretary to the prime minister of New Zealand has announced a new trade agreement with the United States.
> BROADCASTING: The under-secretary to New Zealand's prime minister has announced a new trade agreement with the United States.

Do not substitute titles for names without first making sure that the name itself won't mean anything to the listener and that the title is more important than the name.

Be careful about running too many titles and names closely together; it will only be confusing. Consider the following:

> Secretary of Interior Roger B. Hodges announced that William Jarvis, chairman of U-S Steel, had succeeded Ralph J. Cordiner, chairman of General Electric, as chairman of the president's Business Advisory Committee.

A sentence like that is jarring and totally confusing. The average listener will get absolutely nothing out of the item; there's just too much information in too short a time.

Never refer in your copy to "the former" or "the latter." These words are only useful in print where the reader can look back to see what you are referring to. In broadcast writing, this is impossible and asking the listener to do so will only lead to confusion and frustration.

NAMING THE SOURCE

To maintain radio and television's role as a credible source for news, it is essential that the writer tell the listener the source of information. The writer must be sure that there is no confusion in the listener's mind as to whether the newscaster is speaking personally or for a news source.

Because of the characteristics of the broadcast medium, it is confusing to the listener to hear the source for a statement at the end of that statement. To make the source perfectly clear, experienced radio-TV writers generally place the source first instead of in the middle or at the end of the sentence, as is done by newspapers. There are four general rules to follow until you are thoroughly familiar with the demands of broadcast journalism:

1. Never start a story with a startling statement and then add the source at the end. The listener in his excitement may miss it. Be particularly careful about leading with statements that may mislead your listeners:

> POOR: "This means all-out war with the Soviet Union." At least that's the opinion of Congressman Ron Dellums who appeared before the House Armed Services Committee today.
> BETTER: Congressman Ron Dellums told the House Armed Services Committee today, and these are his exact words: "This means all out war with the Soviet Union."

2. Avoid identifying the source of the statement within the sentence, unless it is essential to break up long quotations.

> POOR: "The only way to end the war," said the president, "is to reach a mutual agreement with the enemy over the disposition of the neutral areas."
> BETTER: The president said, and we quote: "The only way to end the war is to reach a mutual agreement with the enemy over the disposition of the neutral areas."

3. Avoid leaving the name of the source for the end of the statement. By then it may be missed by many listeners. It is also difficult for the listener to know what part of the sentence is the direct quote if the source for the statement comes last.

> POOR: "Last night's narcotics raid was the result of six-months undercover investigation by our department into the widespread use of hard drugs in local high schools," said County Sheriff Jack McIntyre.
> BETTER: County Sheriff Jack McIntyre said, and we quote, "Last night's narcotics raid was the result of six-months under-cover investigation by our department into the widespread use of hard drugs in local high schools."

4. Unless it is awkward, always try to have the source of your information at the beginning of the sentence so your listener is clear as to the credibility of your story.

> POOR: The number of oil slicks along the Pacific coast in the past year is the highest recorded since such records were kept, said University of California-Berkeley biologist Robert Waldman.
> BETTER: A biologist at the University of California-Berkeley, Robert Waldman, says the number of oil slicks along the Pacific coast this year is the highest recorded since such records were kept.

VARIETY IN NAMING THE SOURCE

Obviously, if all your writing were restricted to the rules of the style guide, it would very quickly become dull and trite. Variety is essential. But at the same time, there are certain errors which must be avoided.

A good technique in naming the source for a number of quotations, instead of just repeating the name, is to use each quote as an opportunity to supply additional information. The following example shows one way of doing it:

> *One of Hollywood's most successful screenwriters,* Julie Gianelli, accused the film industry of being hostile towards creative, intelligent women.
>
> *A four-time Academy award nominee,* she told the California Select Committee on Job Discrimination that she had lost many jobs because she was female.
>
> Gianelli, *best known for her box office blockbuster "Wife's Night Out,"* claimed it's still almost impossible for a woman to succeed in Hollywood, unless, and these are her exact words, "she has a good-looking body and is willing to follow orders from her male superiors."

Notice that your listeners have not only learned about Gianelli's opinions, they have also found out about her qualifications.

This technique is a very handy one to use, but there are certain pitfalls which should be avoided. Note the following sentence which strives for variety but ends up merely confusing the listener:

> The chairman of the subcommittee ordered the hearing room cleared of the noisy protestors. Senator Edward Kennedy told the audience he would not tolerate further interruptions.

It doesn't necessarily follow that all your listeners know that Senator Kennedy is, in fact, the chairman of the subcommittee; it is highly probable that most of them do not. Thus, a sentence like this merely frustrates rather than informs. Why not try it this way if you want variety:

> The chairman of the subcommittee ordered the hearing room cleared of the noisy protestors. Chairman Edward Kennedy . . . who had called the investigation at the request of the president . . . told the audience he would not tolerate further interruptions.

Another example may help to clear up any confusion you have:

> A spokesman for the tire manufacturers drew a sharp attack from the chairman. William Bryant said he was tired of hearing testimony. . . .

At this point, ask yourself, who is William Bryant? Is he the spokesman or the chairman? If you are confused, think of your poor audience—they must be totally lost. Why not write the same sentence this way to clear up the ambiguity:

A spokesman for the tire manufacturers drew a sharp attack from chairman William Bryant who said he was tired of hearing testimony. . . .

See how much simpler it now is to follow the story—there is no doubt as to who Bryant is.

ATTRIBUTION

So far I have been talking mainly about the rules for quoting sources. But is it always necessary to give attribution? When can you leave out the source?

Obviously, if there is any question about the credibility of a statement, then attribution is a must. But, in general, the move is definitely towards cutting down the number of times the source is given.

Too much attribution slows the pace of the story. It gets in the way of the action, the color, and often confuses rather than clarifies.

The most obvious place to cut down on attribution is in the writing of ''official'' pronouncements from government offices. As an example, here's a story as it appeared in a newspaper:

U.S. Secretary of State George Shultz today said this country will support a resolution to be introduced into the UN Security Council next week by France to seek total disarmament in the Middle East. Shultz made the announcement to reporters during his weekly news conference in Washington.

Because this is an official announcement, it could be written without attribution in the lead:

The U.S. will support a French resolution to seek total disarmament in the Middle East which will be introduced into the U.N. Security Council next week. Secretary of State George Shultz made the announcement this morning to reporters during his weekly news conference in Washington.

The radio-TV writer should postpone attribution in a story only when there is no question of the credibility of the source. For example, if the president announces he will make a speech to Congress, it is not necessary in the lead to write ''The president says he will. . . .'' It is sufficient to say, ''The president will make a speech to Congress.''

As was pointed out before, the *name* of the source (especially in foreign news) is often less important than their title or position:

POOR: Sir Georges Avedon, under-secretary to the minister of defense for Great Britain, said today his country will. . . .
BETTER: Great Britain's under-secretary of defense says his country will. . . .
BEST: Great Britain will (leaving source understood). . . .

While it is permissible to leave out the source for ''official'' news, it is essential that you attribute all statements of opinion—especially when there may be doubt as to their credibility:

POOR: American auto manufacturers are the major stumbling blocks to establishing proper pollution controls in this country.

BETTER: The director of Ecology Action, Incorporated today charged American auto makers with being the major stumbling blocks to establishing proper. . . .

In the second sentence, there is no longer any question in the listener's mind as to whether the attack on the auto makers is your editorial comment or the opinion of someone else.

In addition, naming the source can often make the difference in the newsworthiness of a story. If General Motors is accused of poor quality control by a member of a consumer group, the story is less "important" than if the same charge comes from the president of the United States.

SAID AND ITS SYNONYMS

The beginning writer will sooner or later run into the problem of too many "he saids" in his stories. Concerned about using the same phrase over and over again, the writer searches vainly for synoyms for *said*. This search can often lead into troubled water because, no matter what some experts say, there are a number of words that just don't have the same connotation as the word *said*.

The word *said* is very often the best you can use and don't hesitate to repeat it if necessary. Its use has become an acceptable convention and few listeners will object to its overuse, especially if synonyms cloud the true meaning of the story.

Many times you will feel the urge to use words like *added, asserted, averred, stated,* etc., as substitutes for *said*. Don't. They do not have the same meaning. To say that a speaker "went on to say," or that he "added" indicates to the listener that the statement was as an afterthought.

If you feel you have to use a substitute for *said,* choose one that adds accurate description or color to your story.

POOR: The mayor *said* in a speech to the Rotary Club this morning she will support the city's drive for cleaner streets.
BETTER: The mayor *promised* the Rotary Club this morning she would support the city's drive for cleaner streets.

Substituting forceful verbs, as was done in the above example, is a good technique but care should be exercised against changing the meaning of the sentence. In the second sentence you would not want to use the word *disclosed* instead of *promised* because it has a different meaning. It indicates that the mayor was revealing some secret information or feeling she had not publicly admitted before.

By the way, the use of the word *add* is another writing pitfall that often traps the beginner.[7] The word should only be used in place of *said* when the second statement does, in fact, amplify, expand, or illuminate the first statement.

POOR: The police chief *declared* [why not *said . . . declared* is a bit formal] crime statistics for the city show a decrease in armed robbery. Storeowners, he *added* have suffered fewer dollar losses in the past month than for the same period last year.

Added is improperly used in the example. The last statement does not add anything to the first sentence; it is merely a continuation. So why not write it that way:

BETTER: The police chief *said* crime statistics for the city show a decrease in armed robbery. Storeowners, he *pointed out* have suffered fewer dollar losses in the past month than for the same period last year.

DIRECT QUOTATIONS

Complete reporting also requires the use of direct quotes, which leads to another problem. How can you handle direct quotes, since the listener can't see quotation marks? It would be possible to say "quote-unquote" before and after every direct quotation. But that technique interrupts the flow of the story and jars the listener. Fortunately for you and your audience, there is an easier, more pleasant way of including direct quotes in your stories.[8]

While it is impossible to tell you how to handle every situation, there are some general guidelines which will go a long way towards helping handle direct quotes with a minimum of effort:

1. Do not use long direct quotes. It is impossible for a listener to follow a long, complex statement. It is much more effective to break them up into indirect quotes by paraphrasing the source.
2. If it is necessary to use a long quote, break it up by naming the source a number of times during the quote.
3. Always indicate to the audience exactly when the quoted material begins and ends. But avoid, if possible, the use of *quote* and *unquote*.

Let's look at each of the guidelines in detail.

The use of long, direct quotes is appropriate for the print media. In radio-television writing the practice leads to awkward and confusing copy. The following example would wreak havoc in the listener's mind:

NEWSPAPER: Warren Stevens, director of College Housing, said, "The main problem we face in our college housing is the lack of appropriate safeguards to ensure our students that the apartments and houses they rent

---

[7] For more common writing errors, see Appendix B, p. 123.
[8] See Appendix A, Style Guide, p. 115.

during the school year will measure up to at least minimum health and
safety standards as established by the state health department last year.''
BROADCASTING: The director of College Housing, Warren Stevens,
said the major problem his office faces regarding college housing is the
lack of appropriate safeguards to ensure that apartments students rent will
meet minimum health and safety standards. Stevens pointed out that these
requirements were set by the state health department last year.

Notice how I have paraphrased the long quote (rule 1) and broken it up into two
sentences bridged by a second identification of the source (rule 2).

If you can't use "quote-unquote," how do you tell the audience you are
reading a direct quote from a second source? You do it the same way for radio
and television that you do in conversation. When you talk to someone, you don't
say "quote-unquote" when you are passing along statements from a second
party. You use phrases such as *in his words, as he put it,* or *what he called.* The
list is endless, but these phrases *plus* your inflection indicate to your listeners
where the quote begins and ends. An example might make this technique clearer:

POOR: The president of General Motors said—quote—our company is
spending millions attempting to solve the problems of air pollution caused
by gasoline engines—unquote.
BETTER: The president of General Motors said, and these are his exact
words: "Our company is spending millions attempting to solve the problems of air pollution caused by gasoline engines."

It is even better to avoid the use of direct quotes. In the above examples,
there is no real reason for quoting the president of General Motors directly—so
why not simply paraphrase his statements. Direct quotes should only be used
when it is essential that you give your audience the exact language of the statement:

The president of General Motors pointed out his company is
spending millions of dollars attempting to solve the problems of air pollution caused by gasoline engines.

On occasion you may run into a direct quote that attaches a label to someone or something. For example, a senator may call the president's State of the
Union message an "historical document" while another may label it an "evasive
statement which avoids confronting the nation's problems." Instead of using
direct quotations, it is possible to write your story in such a way so that listeners
will understand that you are quoting the source, not editorializing:

The senator called the president's message "an historical document." On the other side of the aisle, however, another senator described
the State of the Union speech as an "evasive statement," one which—in
the senator's words—"avoids confronting the nation's problems."

When you are forced to use a long quotation that is impossible to paraphrase, it is essential that you insert a phrase that identifies the source every three

or four sentences to remind the audience that you are reading a direct quote. For example:

> The senator went on to say. . . .
> The senator continued. . . .
> Turning to another topic. . . .
> The senator added. . . .

There is another point to remember when dealing with quotations. Be careful where you place them; use them in full sentences or not at all. If you are careless, you might create this confusing statement which recently cropped up in a radio newscast:

> The governor told newsmen, "*I* will do exactly what I've been doing—nothing more, nothing less."

Read that sentence out loud and you will immediately hear the confusion which can result. The audience, unable to "see" the quotation marks, might think the "I" refers to the newscaster, not to the governor. Using half quotations of this sort is simply lazy writing. Why not write it this way and clear up any possible confusion:

> The governor told newsmen *he* will do exactly what he's been doing—nothing more, nothing less.

Sometimes the use of half quotations can border on the ludicrous. There was another broadcaster, reading a story referring to the confession of a female murderer. The script read: "She said, 'I did it.' " (She didn't say that; she said *she* did it.)

CONTRACTIONS

The various techniques discussed so far will give the audience a clearer understanding of the day's news. All of them mirror to some degree the basics of *conversational* language. The use of contractions (*don't* for *do not, doesn't* for *does not,* etc.) heightens the similarity between broadcasting and conversation. It is perfectly acceptable conversational style to use contractions, and so it is also acceptable braodcast style. The rule then, is to use as *many* contractions as logically fit into your copy.

When we are talking we seldom say "he will" or "I am" or "he is." We say "he'll" or "I'm" or "he's." Since broadcasting tries for the informal, your writing should be liberally sprinkled with these contracted forms, such as:

He's instead of *he is*
He'd instead of *he would*
He'll instead of *he will*
They're instead of *they are*
They'll instead of *they will*

Don't instead of *do not*
Won't instead of *will not*
Doesn't instead of *does not*
Isn't instead of *is not*

In the following examples, notice how the *verbal* sound flow of the newspaper copy is improved by substituting the proper contractions:

NEWSPAPER: Sources in Washington said today Congress *will not* approve the president's latest demand for a $5 billion cutback in the federal welfare program. The president told reporters today *he will* make a personal appearance before a joint congressional session sometime next week to seek the welfare program cuts. The Senate *will not* begin hearings on the measure until next month, and experts *do not* expect any funds to be chopped from the program. Meanwhile the Speaker of the House told newsmen *he is* sure the *House will* back the White House in seeking the cuts.

BROADCASTING: Sources in Washington say Congress *won't* approve the president's latest demand for a five billion dollar cutback in the federal welfare program. The president told reporters today *he'll* make a personal appearance before a joint congressional session sometime next week to seek the welfare program cuts. The Senate *won't* begin hearings on the measure until next month, and experts *don't* expect any funds to be chopped from the program. Meanwhile, the speaker of the House told newsmen he's sure the *House'll* back the White House in seeking the cuts.

Just a word of caution. Don't get carried away with contractions. There are times when you will want to say "did not" instead of "didn't" for emphasis. It is impossible to spell out when you will want to avoid contractions; it depends on the mood of the story and its subject matter.

You should not use contractions inside direct quotes if the original quote did not use them. The speaker had some reason for using the words he chose, and you should not change them in any manner.

COLOR

Because broadcasting involves a great deal of showmanship (unfortunately), newswriters must use attention-getting devices throughout their copy; and one of the best is color.

Conversation is more colorful, more picturesque than the written word. When we speak to someone, we are more likely to use forceful verbs, descriptive adjectives and short sentences. A good news story will include these same ingredients to paint more colorful, meaningful word pictures. This is especially true in radio where your audience cannot see what you are describing; they rely on you to draw them a sound image of the news event.

There is no better way of getting color into your copy than through active verbs. They are more effective than the easier to use adjectives because they create a feeling of action.

When you write your news stories, never forget that you are writing about humans—their trials, their emotions, their faults, their inhumanity. These events have emotional impact. Often they are not "nice" stories. There is nothing pleasant about the killing of 100 innocent persons in an airplane crash. If the story demands strong language (not profanity), then use it.

When you write, get some feeling into your writing. Use verbs that tell the story. Avoid adjectives if you can; they weaken the flow of the story. If you can find a verb that can take the place of an adjective, use it.

The use of short, simple sentences goes a long way to energizing your story. Try to avoid the use of complex dependent and independent clauses; they merely confuse the listener. Try to make sense out of this paragraph:

> Using Senator Robert Knight's familiar, and often successful technique—a television interview—California Republican Congressman Henry Johnson charged—in a voice strained with contempt—that. . . .

Another effective way of getting more color into your writing is to avoid the negative aspect of a story. The beginning sentences of a story that focus on the negative may be dull. It's much like telling the listener that nothing is going to happen. The skilled writer will try to translate the negative into the positive:

POOR: The president told newsmen today *he will not oppose* the attempt by Congress to change the voting requirements for Negroes in the south.
BETTER: The president told newsmen today he *will refuse* to oppose the attempt by Congress to change the voting requirements for Negroes in the south.
POOR: Inside sources say the county grand jury *won't* bring criminal charges against 12 persons arrested last week on various drug charges.
BETTER: Inside sources say the county grand jury *will drop* plans to bring criminal charges against 12 persons arrested last week on various charges.
POOR: The governor revealed today he *won't go* to Washington tomorrow to seek presidential intervention to get that 9-billion dollar defense contract for California's missile industry.
BETTER: The governor revealed today he is *cancelling* plans to go to Washington to seek presidential intervention to get that 9-billion dollar defense contract for California's missile industry.

Obviously, it is unwise and impossible to convert all negative leads into the positive. Again, it is left to your judgment, but it can be done frequently and effectively.

One other fault common with beginning writers, and one that makes for dull writing, is the use of the passive voice rather than the more action oriented active voice.

In the active voice sentence, you have the subject doing something: "John hit the ball." In the passive voice, you have something being done to the subject:

"The ball was hit by John." Admittedly these examples are a bit simpleminded, but the principle also holds true for more complex constructions.

POOR: The housing legislation, which was passed by the Senate this morning, will be acted on by the House later this week.

This entire sentence is in the passive voice (and emphasizes an old angle). Putting in the active voice gives the story a feeling of action:

BETTER: Later this week the House will act on housing legislation the Senate approved this morning.

Be constantly on the lookout for the passive voice—it dulls your copy:

PASSIVE: The bill was passed by Congress.
ACTIVE: Congress passed the bill.

PASSIVE: The car was crushed by the truck.
ACTIVE: The truck crushed the car.

PASSIVE: Signed into law by the governor, the bill takes effect tomorrow.
ACTIVE: The governor signed the bill which takes effect tomorrow.

PASSIVE: The suspect is being questioned by police.
ACTIVE: The police are questioning the suspect.

Although color is essential to a good news story, sometimes too much color can be confusing to your audience. A particular danger crops up when you use adjectives, especially strings of them to modify one subject. The phrase, "the handsome, rugged building supervisor," can be a confusing image to grasp. What is handsome and rugged; the building or the supervisor?

WRITING FOR THE EAR

So far I have been talking about the various parts of a news story written for radio and television. Now it's time to look at the story in its entirety.

Again I must emphasize that broadcast writing is writing for the ear. Listeners do not have the luxury of going back and "rehearing" what they missed the first time. It is essential that your stories be crystal clear. It is imperative that your writing be as simple as possible.

As you write each story remember that you are writing for a listener that may be half-deaf with the maturity of a nine-year-old. Your stories must be simple enough to reach this listener. Yet, at the same time, they must be intellectual enough to reach the 45-year old corporation executive or the college professor.

I am not suggesting that your writing be couched in fifth grade terminology. All I'm saying is that if you err, it is better to err on the side of simplicity. The banking executive won't get too upset if the story is told in elementary terms, but your half-deaf mental incompetent will be completely confused if your writing is complex.

What you must accept is the hard fact that only a small segment of your audience uses the other media (newspaper, magazines, books, etc.) to supplement your reports. The major share of your audience unfortunately relies almost completely on the broadcast media for its news. If they don't get it from radio and television news, then they don't get it at all. Hopefully this dependency on the electronic media as a single news source will change in the future, but all present indications point to the fact that the trend will continue and grow stronger.

So it is your obligation to put the day's news in terms that the "average" person-in-the-street will understand and *listen* to.

If you read aloud to some friend a news story from your local newspaper, he will probably miss most of the major points the first time through. He just cannot cope with the complex style that is the hallmark of most newspaper writing. Rewrite the same story in simple everyday language and your friend will have a much easier time of it.

For example, a newspaper account of a battle action might read:

An estimated force of 1350 pro-Marxist rebels struck hard at government positions in various locations throughout the cease-fire zone in Angola yesterday. Heavily damaged, were numerous government fuel depots, trucks and light armored vehicles. Rebel losses were described as minor.

The average person might start his account this way:

Boy, that sure was some battle yesterday in Angola!

Obviously, you wouldn't write your news story in such an off-hand manner. But you could blend the formal newspaper approach with conversational style to create this version:

Pro-Marxist rebels struck hard at government troops in Angola yesterday. Some 13-hundred rebels attacked in various locations throughout the cease-fire zone. Numerous government fuel depots, trucks and light armored vehicles were heavily damaged. Rebel losses were minor.

The easiest way to simplify your stories is to simplify your sentences. Most of our everyday sentences are simple declarative statements—subject, verb and object. Your writing should reflect this practice.

But don't get carried away. You can fall into the habit of short, jerky, disconnected thoughts, and sentences. Your writing should *flow* smoothly from one thought to the next; from one sentence to the next; from one paragraph to the next.

One good technique for achieving this compromise between *flow* and simple construction is talking to your typewriter while you write. Read each sentence out loud as you pound the keys. And after you finish writing a paragraph or two, go back and read it again to make doubly sure it makes sense and *flows*.

Many beginning writers find it necessary to prepare a rough draft of the story before they type the final version. This may work for preparing essays or other leisurely forms of writing. But when you are writing a news story against the pressure of a time deadline, you simply cannot afford to waste effort producing a rough draft.

You must train to write the final version the first time. Before you begin to write, take a moment or two and think about the approach you will use, what you want to say, and how you are going to say it. Once the story shapes up in your mind then, and only then, should you begin to write.

The only way to learn this skill is to practice writing. It is impossible to learn how to write without spending time at it. After all, you wouldn't expect to learn to play the piano by just reading a book, so how can you expect to learn to write without hours of practice, correction, review, and more practice.

There are a few specific *don'ts* which should be learned:

1. Don't start a sentence with long, modifying clauses:

POOR: Despite complaints from student militant groups and urgings from conservative forces for more stringent action against campus violence, the governor is refusing to issue a policy statement.
BETTER: The governor is refusing to issue a policy statement on the current problem of campus violence despite complaints from student militant groups and urging from conservative forces for more stringent action.

2. Don't leave clauses or attribution dangling at the end of a sentence:

POOR: There are now more than four radio receivers for every American man, woman, and child according to a report released recently by the U-S Census Bureau.
BETTER: A report recently released by the U-S Census Bureau says there are more than four radio receivers for every man, woman, and child in America.

3. Don't place a lot of confusing clauses between the subject and the verb:

POOR: The President, obviously upset over the refusal of Congress to approve his call for deep cuts in social security benefits, says he will appear on national radio and television tonight to plead for public support.
BETTER: The President will appear on national radio and television tonight to plead for public support after Congress ignored his demand for cuts in social security benefits.

4. Don't use strings of dependent clauses. Make separate sentences:

POOR: The mayor of San Francisco, who took office less than a year ago, surprised reporters by announcing he would not be a candidate for re-election because he feels the public has lost faith in his administration over its handling of the recent municipal workers strike.

BETTER: The mayor of San Francisco surprised reporters this afternoon by telling them he would not be a candidate for re-election. He said he had decided against seeking a second term because he thinks the public has lost faith in his administration. The mayor said the public is upset over the way he handled the recent city worker strike. The mayor has been in office less than a year.

THE LEAD

When you start a journey, you must take the first step. The same applies to news stories. The first thing you must write is the lead. If you do not catch the interest of your audience with your first sentence or two, you have lost them for the rest of the story.

Actually, the use of the term *lead* in broadcast journalism is misleading (no pun intended). The term originated with newspapers. It was developed to suit the mechanics of that medium. It was a specialized and somewhat artificial method of getting into the first paragraph of a newspaper story all the essential information about the event. This was done to attract the reader's attention and to allow copy editors to cut the story at the end of the first paragraph and still retain the "meat" of the item.

However, if broadcast writers try to cram the "who, what, when, where, why and how" of an event into the first paragraph, the story becomes cumbersome, awkward to read and very confusing.

In the early days of radio news, news reports consisted simply of reading the local newspaper *verbatim,* a practice still common at many small stations. But announcers soon realized that it was impossible to read the fact-crammed leads and the awkward newspaper style. Copy written for the eye just could not be delivered for the ear in an understandable fashion.

So over a period of time radio writers developed their own style of lead writing, one that caught the listener's attention, eased him into the story with one or two important facts and prepared him for other facts which followed.

The philosophy of the radio, or "soft," lead is fairly simple. The ability of the human brain to receive and understand audio information is limited in terms of the amount of material that can be assimilated over a given period of time. And, more importantly the brain must be alerted and prepared to "hear" this information.

So it is the function of the "soft" lead to alert the listener that something is going to be said that is important. But that alert must be kept fairly simple and interesting to arouse that interest and maintain it.

There is another important reason for the "soft" lead. Listening to the radio, unlike reading the newspaper, is often done in a subconscious manner. People listen while they are busy doing something else. Listeners may be daydreaming, eating, driving a car or even reading a newspaper. They only half listen until something is said that grabs their interest and makes them want to devote their full attention to the story.

Users of all media—print and broadcast—select what they want to read or hear on the basis of their own needs or interests. No matter how important a story might seem to you, if your audience hears nothing in it that involves them in some way, they won't pay attention to it.

Radio news, like printed news, competes for the attention of its listeners. To get attention, stories must be interesting, colorful, easy to understand, and above all, put in terms that will make the item *important* and *meaningful* to listeners in terms of their particular needs.

The only way to determine those needs is to know the audience you are writing for. If the audience is primarily rural in nature, you would select and edit copy in terms of agricultural interests. On the other hand, the audience might be composed mainly of middle-class, white collar workers situated in a suburban area. This audience needs a different approach to the news from its rural counterparts. Each audience is different and for a news operation to be successful it must be planned with its audience in mind.

As you write each story remember your listeners and ask "What is there about this event that will interest them?" "What do my listeners consider important . . . what do they need to know about the event I am reporting?"

Since people listen to the radio in a half-hearted manner for the most part, it is essential to snare the undivided attention of your listeners without giving them facts they will need later on to understand the news.

The newspaper writer can cram all the information into a lead and rely on the headline to grab the reader's eye; and, if something is not understood the reader can go back and check the story again.

The broadcast writer must always remember that listeners may not hear those first few words because they weren't paying attention. Therefore, it is essential that you "warmup" the listeners by telling them what is coming next.

Not only must you alert listeners to pay attention, but you must make the story interesting enough to make them want to pay attention. Fail to do this, and you have lost them for the story and perhaps the entire newscast.

The lead sentence in a radio news story is much like a newspaper headline. It demands attention and prepares for what is to follow.

I have already discussed the guidelines concerning the use of names and titles, and nothing would be gained by repeating that advice here. Suffice to say that the rules governing the starting of a sentence with a name apply even more to the starting of a story. The only exception would be when the name is so familiar to your audience that it acts as a cue to what is to follow.

POOR: Robert Martin, a professor of mass communications at Chico State College, will spend a year in Africa under a grant from the United Nations.

BETTER: A Chico State College mass communications professor, Robert Martin, will spend a year in Africa under a grant from the United Nations.

POOR: Miss Stephanie Bradley of Boise, Idaho, was selected as this year's Miss America last night in Atlantic City, New Jersey.

BETTER: A Boise, Idaho, girl . . . Miss Stephanie Bradley . . . was selected as this year's Miss America last night in Atlantic City, New Jersey.

I also recommend that you don't start your story with statistics. Since listeners are not "ready" for the information, they will miss it completely and spend the rest of the story wondering what you are talking about.

POOR: Twelve persons are dead and 30 others seriously injured following the latest outbreak of violence in the riot-torn streets of Beirut.

BETTER: The latest outbreak of violence in the riot-torn streets of Beirut has left twelve dead and 30 others seriously injured.

POOR: One-thousand high-school volunteers rang some 10-thousand doorbells last night and collected over 35-hundred dollars for UNICEF.

BETTER: Local high school students did their good deed last night as some one-thousand volunteers rang some 10-thousand doorbells and collected over 35-hundred dollars for UNICEF.

There are a number of specific techniques a broadcast writer can use to "warmup" an audience. Which one to use in a particular situation can only be learned through experience.

However, one useful approach—especially when you have a number of items relating to the same event—is the "round-up" or "umbrella" lead. This alerts the listener that there are a number of related stories to follow.

For example:

From Maine to Georgia, the East coast is still shivering after 10 days of below-zero temperature that has brought life to a standstill, especially in Boston, New York, and Washington. All three cities have been declared federal disaster areas after freezing rains destroyed power systems and water pipes, leaving millions stranded in dark, unheated apartments and homes.

In Boston, more than five thousand people had to be rescued from stalled trains in the city's subway tunnels after ice collapsed the main power cables for the system.

In New York, traffic stopped dead after the traffic lights went dark. The massive snarl is expected to last at least another 24 hours until the lights can be repaired.

Meanwhile, hundreds of streets and highways in the nation's capital are buried under at least a foot of mud left by the flooding Potomac River. Clean-up efforts are underway, but it will be another week before traffic will be able to flow easily through Washington D.C.

The Memorial Day weekend is over and the state highway death toll is at an all-time high as 23 deaths were recorded during the 48-hour period.

In Macon, three persons died when their small truck ran off the highway. . . .

Six teenagers died after their car was struck by a train. . . .

A family of four perished when their car was struck headon . . . [and the rest of the story would continue to describe each accident if they were of local interest.]

Sometimes the "umbrella" lead is not appropriate. In that case, you might try what is called a "throw-away" lead. This is a lead sentence which "sets up" the listener for the story. It is not really the true lead which is usually the second sentence or paragraph; hence the name "throw-away." For example:

The county board of supervisors surprised everyone . . . including themselves it seems . . . by voting unanimously to turn down a request to construct a massive housing complex on the banks of the Chico River.

By a vote of six to nothing, the board said no to contractor William Davis who had sought permission to build some one thousand homes along the river banks. Speaking for the board, Supervisor Thomas Roas said—and we quote—"Such a project would be detrimental to the health of the river and would increase the chances of pollution . . . a situation we cannot allow."

OR

An east bay newspaper editor has strongly criticized the recent action by radical groups against the University of California-Berkeley.

Appearing on CBS's "Face the Nation," Oakland Tribune editor Lee Merryl charged that radicals are, in her words, "deliberately provoking the University of California into a police action. . . ."

OR

The state may be in financial hot water in the near future if a local grocery store owner wins his court hearing seeking to overthrow the state's right to collect sales tax.

The store owner . . . Zachary David . . . has filed suit in superior court against the state board of equalization charging that the state is violating the constitution by collecting sales tax. David forced the court hearing by refusing to pay his sales tax last month.

You will notice that in the above examples the first sentence alerts the listener to the rest of the story. The details of the event (the *true* lead) do not appear until the second paragraph. The story would make sense without the first sentence; its only function is to serve as an attention grabber.

Writing an effective lead is probably the most important aspect of the writer's job. If you lose a listener because of a poor lead, it is possible that we will have lost him for the rest of the newscast.

It is essential that the lead "hook" the listener. This can only be done by making your leads as interesting, vital, and *local* as possible. The last requirement, as I have been stressing over and over again, is the most important. There is hardly a story that cannot be rewritten to emphasize the local angle and to tell the audience why they should care about knowing the details of an event.

There is one caution that should be exercised when writing your leads (and your stories, for that matter). You must be careful about inserting editorial judgments disguised as interpretations. You should avoid such phrases as, "There's good news tonight from the capitol. . . ." What may be good news for one part of your audience may be, and probably is, bad news for some other section.

COUPLING PINS

One of the advantages broadcast journalism has over newspapers is its ability to tie stories together. Radio-television writers create this cohesive whole by using "coupling pins" or "transes" as they are commonly called in newsroom slang.

A "trans" is simply a word or phrase that carries the audience smoothly from one news item to the next. It may be written at the end of one story or at the beginning of the next. It may even be pencilled in during the final editing process after the story order has been decided by the editor.

Coupling pins are "throw-away" material. They can be left out of the newscast without being missed. But if they are used skillfully, they can add to the understanding of the news by giving the listener the impression that the entire newscast has been integrated with thought and planning.

Effective transition statements give a perspective, a time reference, a point of departure against which to view the "total fabric" of the day's events.

There is some disagreement among broadcast journalists ever using "transes." Some feel they are an artificial device, while others use them constantly without logical consistency or concern for the *flow* of the copy.

Actually, such coupling pins are quite normal in everyday conversation. It is common practice to sprinkle our speech with phrases that link one thought to the next or words that alert our listener about what is coming next. To do this, we use such phrases as *by the way, meanwhile, as you recall, at the same time, however, while that was going on,* etc.

Obviously, many of the phrases we use in conversational language cannot be used in broadcast writing. But there is one bit of advice you can borrow from the "street language." Don't use transitional phrases where they don't logically fit. If you have to strain to put in a trans, don't.

When you are writing coupling pins, look for some common element that links the various items together. It may be geographical, time sequence, activity, historical references—anything to indicate to the listener that there is a thread that draws the stories together.

For example, if you write a story about a nationwide auto-worker strike, you might tie the various reports from around the country in the following manner. The transitions are in bold face italics:

The nationwide walkout by auto workers is in its third week, and according to reports from company officials, it is spreading rapidly. *In Detroit* the big three auto makers—Ford, Chrysler, and General Motors— have shut down all operations. *Meanwhile, word from St. Louis* is that the Ford assembly plant there has laid off 75 percent of its work force and expects to close down completely by next week. *While the auto workers are idle,* there is a chance that the nation's teamsters may also strike. Contracts with shipping firms expire tomorrow at midnight and round-the-clock bargaining sessions have been termed by both sides as unproductive. *The auto strike and the threat of a trucking strike* had an effect on the stock market today which fell more than 15 points in the closing Dow Jones averages. Experts say the unsettled economic conditions of the country are causing the slide. *One of those hardest hit by the slumping market* is billionaire J. Richard Andrews. He has suffered paper losses on his stock holdings of more than 15-million dollars. *Well, the stock market may be in the doldrums* . . . but the San Francisco Giants sure aren't, as they won their 15th game in a row today beating the Los Angeles Dodgers 10–5.

It is possible by careful organization to tie various elements into a single theme (the auto strike and slumping economy) and to carry that theme throughout the broadcast even to the sports report.

It is impossible to list all the possible coupling pins you could write and to lay down specific guidelines for their use. There are too many forms of transitions available; your imagination and creativity are the only limits. But before you use a transition, make sure that you are not forcing the effect. If a coupler does not fit naturally, you will have done more harm than good.

3

Sources of News

SO FAR I HAVE BEEN DEALING with the preparation of news stories; but where does all the raw information come from? The answer is quite simple—news sources. To function properly, you must have a number of reliable news sources which supply your daily fund of information from which you build good news reports. The number and quality of these sources decide the value of the final product.

Even though national and international news organizations are often called "wire services," they have long since abandoned telegraph and telephone cables in favor of satellite delivery which instantly supplies thousands of news clients around the world with an endless stream of words and images.

Associated Press (AP) and United Press International (UPI) are the two major news sources for newspapers, magazines, radio, and television stations in the United States. They are a link with the outside world and provide coverage of events a station could not afford on its own.

Both AP and UPI offer news written specifically for radio (they also provide stories written in newspaper style for the print media) on a 24-hour basis. Each service supplies prepared newscasts, headlines, sports, farm and agricultural news, regional and state news summaries, women's news, features, and, of course, weather.

These world-wide news gathering ventures which service more than six-thousand clients in America alone, had their beginnings in a Boston coffeehouse less than a century ago.[1] There, tavern owner Samuel Topliffe kept a "news ledger" in which he wrote down news reports that arrived from England on the

[1] Rosewater, Victor, *History of Cooperative Newsgathering in the United States*, New York: Appleton, 1930.

latest merchant ship. Boston newspapers, hungry for the latest developments from Europe, were more than willing to spend the time going through his ledger to dig out what sparse facts they could.

But news cooperation as we know it got its start in the 1820s when a group of New York City daily newspapers pooled their resources and a small amount of money to have a small boat go out and meet the incoming ships sailing into New York harbor to get the latest news for all its members simultaneously.

This "combine" later drew up a charter and a table of organization and became a closed group called the New York Associated Press in 1848. And for the next half-century, this group expanded its service and its number of members, until, by the 1890s, it was supplying news by telegraph wire to clients as far away as San Francisco.

In 1898, however, a rival organization, the Western Associated Press based in Chicago, overthrew the New York management to form the present-day Associated Press.

Today, two competing full-service news-gathering organizations are in operation. Their coverage and service extend over the globe, even into communist countries.

The AP is still fully cooperative. It is owned by its *members,* who as stockholders are given full voting privileges in deciding company policy. AP currently services some three-thousand radio and television stations and about 1600 newspapers.

The other giant is UPI which came into existence by the 1958 marriage of the United Press (founded by Scripps-Howard Newspapers in 1907) and the International News Service (started by the Hearst organization in 1909). UPI, unlike AP, is strictly a news supplier. Each *client* pays UPI a sum based on various factors including the size of its market (not the amount of news used) and has no direct voice in company policy. UPI is operated like any other commercial venture, only its product is news and its customers are the various news media.

Both services have two broad systems, their domestic file and world file. The domestic file is sent to American clients, while the world file is transmitted to international members.

The domestic *newspaper* service is based on a "trunk" wire which is the main channel of news to members throughout the country. The "A" wire carries the bulk of general news; and the "B" wire carries any overload from the "A," but basically serves as a regional wire and supplier of lengthy features. It is the "B" wire that is of major interest to broadcasters as this serves as an excellent supplement to the radio wire by providing in-depth regional news reports and lengthy interpretive pieces, two items the radio wire scrimps on.

It should be pointed out that if a broadcast news operation uses the "B" wire, it will be necessary to rewrite the lion's share of its content since it is written in newspaper style. However, this drawback should not deter a conscientious news operation since the "B" wire provides an essential source of more detailed news reports.

In addition to the "A" and "B" newspaper wires, there is the broadcast wire service—the essential and, unfortunately, often the only ingredient in broadcast journalism.

The AP broadcast wire transmits 22 national and international news summaries Monday through Friday, and a slightly fewer number on the weekends. While each newscast is written for five minutes of airtime, additional material is provided within brackets which, if used, extend the air time to ten minutes.

To supply state and regional news, the AP sets aside 22 time periods daily, called "splits," for regional AP bureaus to transmit regional and state developments.

The UPI broadcast wire is a bit more elaborate than its competition, offering six fifteen-minute and 18 five-minute national and international news summaries (called "World News Round-up" and "World in Brief," respectively), seven days a week.

Like AP, UPI sets aside several periods during the day for regional and state splits. And like AP, regional UPI bureaus can extend these periods if local news developments warrant.

In addition to their broadcast wires, UPI and AP offer clients (for an extra charge) an audio service that offers 70 to 75 news inserts daily, each averaging about 45 seconds long. About half of them are "actualities" (the voices and sounds of people and events in the news); the others feature voice reports ("voicers") from newsmen on the scene describing the incident.

The stations subscribing to the audio service are provided with a telephone line that is kept open 24 hours a day. This wire is attached to a tape recorder equipped with a device that turns the machine on whenever a sound comes down the line from UPI or AP. Then when the transmission ends, the recorder shuts itself off.

The schedule and rundown of the audio feed is sent on the broadcast wire several times during the day, listing what each report is about, how many seconds it runs, whether it is an actuality or a voicer, its point of origin, and the "out cue," or the last few words.

The following audio roundup is indicative of AP's audio service.[2] Each feed is numbered consecutively during the day to make it easier for future reference. Each listing includes, reading from left to right: (a) reference number, (b) whether actuality or voices (A or V), (c) length of feed, (d) origin of story, (e) name of person in feed, (f) the out cue, and (g) subject matter of feed:

167-A-18-(A-P CORR. MARK KNOLLER)-"TO ACCEPT"-EXPERTS SURPRISED BY HOW LITTLE BURN DAMAGE THEY SEE ON SHUTTLE DEBRIS.
168-A-25-(MARK KNOLLER)-"SHUTTLE CREW"-SOME SHUTTLE WRECKAGE ARE A GHOSTLY REMINDER OF THE CHALLENGER DISASTER.
ARROW AIR INQUIRY
169-V-26-OTTAWA, CANADA-(NORMAN JACK)-CANADIAN AVIATION

[2] Used by permission of AP.

SAFETY BD. HEARS MORE TESTIMONY THAT ICE ON WING WAS MAJOR
CAUSE OF DEC. CRASH OF ARROW AIR DC-8 AT GANDER.
  170-A-13-(CAPT. JOHN STEEVES, C-P AIR, WHOSE FLIGHT WAS DELAYED
90 MINUTES BECAUSE OF CRASH, W- MBR. OF CANADIAN AVIATION
SAFETY BD.)-"THE WINGS, MM-HMM"-WEATHER CONDITIONS CREATED
ICE COATING ON PLANES THE MORNING OF CRASH. (STEEVES ORDERED
DE-ICING ON HIS OWN PLANE AFTER EXAMINING HIS AIRCRAFT'S WINGS)
  AP-LA-04-09-86 1138 T

    The following audio roundup is indicative of UPI's audio service. It is the
fifth feed of the day. Each is numbered consecutively during a 24-hour cycle to
make future reference easier. Each listing includes, reading from left to right: (a)
reference number, (b) length of feed, (c) whether actuality or voicer, (d) origin
of story, (e) name of person or reporter in feed, (f) subject matter and (g) the
out-cue:

880LR
    NETWORK-5TH ROUNDUP
  4-15 7:10P
  FEED BEGINS WITH CUT 247. AFTER ALL NEW MATERIAL IS FED, THERE
WILL BE A REPEAT MATERIAL FROM THE HOURLY NEWSFEEDS.
    LIBYA
  247 :11 A TRIPOLI (U-P-I CORRESPONDENT, MARIE COLVIN) NOT SURE
WHAT PRINCIPALS WERE INVOLVED IN SECOND NIGHT OF WEAPONS FIRE
IN TRIPOLI (ACTUALLY BOMBED)
  248 :30 A TRIPOLI (COLVIN) HAS CONFIRMATION FROM KHADAFY FAM-
ILY PEDIATRICIAN ON DEATH OF KHADAFY'S FIFTEEN MONTH OLD
ADOPTED DAUGHTER (ANOTHER DAUGHTER)
  249 :12 A TRIPOLI (COLVIN) KHADAFY'S PEDIATRICIAN SAYS KHADA-
FY'S DAUGHTER DIED AT THE HOSPITAL (THE COMPOUND)
  250 :21 A TRIPOLI (COLVIN) DESCRIBES SCENE IN TRIPOLI IN AFTER-
MATH OF SECOND NIGHT OF WEAPONS FIRE (NO HEADLIGHTS)
    SHUTTLE
  251 :47 V-A KENNEDY SPACE CTR (ROB NAVIAS W-RICHARD TRULY,
NASA ASSOC ADMINISTRATOR FOR SPACEFLIGHT) NASA MANAGERS RE-
VIEW SPACE AGENCY INVESTIGATION AS SALVAGE CREW BRING HOME
MORE REMAINS OF CHALLENGER'S ASTRONAUTS
  252 :19 A K-S-C (RICHARD TRULY, NASA ASSOC ADMINISTRATOR FOR
SPACEFLIGHT) PLEASED ABOUT RECOVERY CREWS FINDING THE CRITI-
CAL JOINT FROM CHALLENGER'S RIGHT-HAND SOLID ROCKET BOOSTER
(PARTICULAR PIECE)

253 :23 A K-S-C (WILLIAM GRAHAM, ACTING NASA ADMINISTRATOR)
ASA IS MAKING GOOD PROGRESS IN INTS PROBE OF THE SHUTTLE DI-
STER (WILL REPORT)
  UPI 04-15-86 04:18 PPS

Around the turn of the century, the forerunner of UPI and AP delivered
out ten thousand words a day to their clients by Morse code over miles of
egraph wires. Eighty years later, UPI is sending almost thirteen million words
day via satellite. This unbelievable leap in news information is made possible
 computer technology which can process, transmit, store, and retrieve data
th amazing speed and efficiency.

To make it easier for clients to deal with this information flood, both AP
d UPI allow for custom tailoring monitored by sophisticated, centralized com-
ters to direct the flow of desired information. For the first time, a local radio
tion can order up a daily diet of news specifically designed to meet the needs
 its listeners. This makes it even more essential that news directors and report-
s have a clear image of their audience. Without it, the opportunities offered by
mputerized news services will be wasted.

As an example, notice how UPI is able to offer very narrow choices. Under
e broad topic of entertainment, you can combine twenty-one options into an
finite variety of show business coverage, as the CustomNews National Menu
. 60) indicates.

THE FLASH AND BULLETIN IN CHINA

Work around wire machines for any length of time and sooner or later you
ill experience your first bulletin. When the wire services send a bulletin, a
pecial circuit is tripped which triggers a bell inside the machine. The number of
ll rings signals the urgency of the story. While each wire service and its bu-
aus around the country has its own idea of what constitutes bulletin material,
 you ever hear five bells in a row, you can presume it's something important
d you had better drop what you are doing and go take a look. But five bells
n't top priority. If you should happen to hear twelve bells, then you know that
mething of transcendental importance has occurred. The President has been
ot, war has been declared, etc.

"Flash" is the highest level of news priority. It consists of a few words of
ummary, rather than a news lead (*i.e.,* "President is shot. . ."). It is usually
peated. Next in order of news-worthiness comes the bulletin, which is a one-
aragraph introduction to an unexpected story. It takes priority over everything
xcept a flash. AP's third priority is a "95," which is used to cover good stories,
sually not expected, and consists of several paragraphs.

UPI uses both the flash and the bulletin, but instead of a "95," UPI uses
n "Urgent."

Broadcast Journalism

CustomNews National Menu

All times eastern

#	Item	✔	Time	Code	Notes
89	Broadcast Row			nnvb	
90	National Daybook (Customnews only)			nnvp	
91	Newsphotos (for Newsphoto subscribers)			nnvp	
92	EBS test			zzebs	
93	Radio Network Billboards			nav	
94	For Radio subscribers with newscasts only			nava	
95	ENTERTAINMENT				
96	All entertainment copy, takeouts, features			nne	
97	Bulletins and urgents			nne ... be	
98	Entertainment advisories			nnve	
99 100	Entertainment takeouts—100– to 200-words stand-alone stories			nnet	
101 102	Entertainment features—daily, weekly and annual			neef	Move btw/ 6pm–6am
103	Today in Music			nnefmdt.	Monday–Friday
104	All music charts			nnefmwc.	Fridays
105	Pop Singles-Albums			nnefmwcr	
106	Country & Western			nnefmwcw	
107	Adult Contemporary			nnefmwcp	
108	Black Singles			nnefmwcb	
109	Christian Contemporary			nnefmwcg	
110	Music World			nnefmwm.	Saturdays
111	The Year in Music			nnefmay.	December
112	Top 100 Records of the Year			nnefmat.	
113	Entertainment Today			nnefede.	Monday–Friday
114	Book Corner			nnefbwc.	Saturdays
115	Video Charts (CustomNews only)			nneftd	Mondays
116	Movie Charts (CustomNews only)			nnefewv.	Saturdays
117	FINANCIAL				
118 119	Complete financial report—see separate listing for cash and commodities markets			nnf	
120	Bulletins and urgents			nnf ... bf	
121	Financial advisories			nnvf	
122 123	Financial takeouts—100– to 200-word stand-alone stories			nnft	
124	FINANCIAL HEADLINES				
125 126	All financial headlines—6 one-minute financial news summaries			nnfh	
127	1st Financial Headlines		5:00 am	nnfh.f ..	
128	2nd Financial Headlines		11:30 am	nnfh.m ..	
129	3rd Financial Headlines		1:30 pm	nnfh.o ..	
130	4th Financial Headlines		2:30 pm	nnfh.p ..	
131	5th Financial Headlines		3:30 pm	nnfh.q ..	
132	Final Financial Headlines		5:30 pm	nnfh.s ..	

Reproduced below is a segment of the UPI wire for September 9, 1976 which included a Flash and Bulletin about the death of Mao Tse-Tung. Added are the necessary explanatory notes:

1255

FLASH—MAO TSE-TUNG DEAD
UPI 09-09 03:09 ACD

1256
B U L L E T I N
(MAO)

(TOKYO)—RADIO PEKING REPORTS CHINESE COMMUNIST PARTY CHAIRMAN

MAO TSE-TUNG DIED TODAY.

UPI 09-09 03:09 ACD

For the next seven minutes, while UPI waited for further developments, it resumed sending its usual diet of news. Then at 3:16, it broke in with more details. Note how UPI indicates how the information should be added to the bulletin (XXX today)].

1258
MORE-MAO BULLETIN
XXX TODAY.
THE RADIO PEKING BROADCAST . . . MONITORED IN TOKYO . . . SAID MAO DIED AT 1:10 A-M PEKING TIME . . . SEVERAL HOURS BEFORE THE EVENT WAS ANNOUNCED HE WAS 82.
UPI 09-09 03:16 ACD

Thirteen minutes later, UPI sent more details to be "fed into" its original bulletin item.]

1261
MORE-MAO BULLETIN
XXX WAS 82.
MAO HAD BEEN REPORTED ILL AND RECENTLY STOPPED MEETING FOREIGN DIGNITARIES IN PEKING.
FORMER PRESIDENT RICHARD NIXON WAS THE LAST PROMINENT AMERICAN CITIZEN TO MEET MAO. NIXON VISITED PEKING LAST FEBRUARY, SHORTLY AFTER FORMER PREMIER CHOU EN-LAI DIED.

THE LAST FOREIGN DIGNITARY TO MEET MAO WAS PAKISTANI PRIME
MINISTER ZULFIKAR ALI BHUTTO LAST MAY 27TH.
    UPI 09-09 03:29 ACD

*[It took almost a half-hour after its "flash" for UPI to prepare a complete version of the
death story. Note the instruction from UPI to "insert as lead item in first World News
Roundup.]*

H264
    (MAO SUB)
    (TOKYO)—AILING CHINESE COMMUNIST PARTY CHAIRMAN MAO TSE-
TUNG (MOW TZUH-DOONG) DIED TODAY IN PEKING AT THE AGE OF 82.
FIRST NEWS OF THE EVENT TO REACH THE OUTSIDE WORLD WAS A
BROADCAST BY RADIO PEKING . . . MONITORED IN TOKYO . . . THAT SAID
MAO DIED AT 1:10 A-M PEKING TIME.
    THE DEATH OF MAO, WHO SUCCESSFULLY UNIFIED CHINA TO A DE-
GREE NEVER ACHIEVED BEFORE, FOLLOWED BY SEVEN MONTHS THAT OF
PREMIER CHOU EN-LAI (JOH EHN-LIGH).
    THE CHINESE COMMUNIST LEADER WAS REPORTED IN POOR HEALTH
SINCE THE START OF THE YEAR AND FOREIGN VISITORS TO PEKING WHO
MET HIM REPORTED HE SOMETIMES NEEDED A MEMO TO CARRY OUT

    MAO'S DEATH IS EXPECTED TO INTENSIFY A POWER STRUGGLE WITHIN
THE CHINESE HIERARCHY. HIS PASSING CAME CLOSELY ON THE HEELS OF
A BITTER CAMPAIGN IN CHINA AGAINST FORMER DEPUTY PREMIER TENG
HSIAO-PING (TEHNG SOW-PEENG) WHO HAS BEEN STRIPPED OF ALL HIS
GOVERNMENT AND PARTY POSTS.
    AS MAO GREW MORE FRAIL IN RECENT MONTHS, FEWER AND FEWER
FOREIGN VISITORS SAW HIM. FORMER PRESIDENT RICHARD NIXON WAS
THE LAST PROMINENT AMERICAN CITIZEN TO MEET MAO . . . IN FEBRU-
ARY. THE LAST FOREIGN DIGNITARY TO MEET MAO WAS PAKISTANI
PRIME MINISTER ZULFIKAR ALI BHUTTO ON MAY 27TH.
    -0-
    (INSERT AS LEAD ITEM IN FIRST WORLD NEWS ROUNDUP)
    UPI 09-09 03:45, ACD[3]

UPDATES

Rewriting stories to include recent information and provide "up-dates" is
a skill honed to perfection by wire service writers facing the problem of preparing numerous versions of copy during a normal news cycle. An excellent exam-

ple of this process can be studied by examining the techniques used by UPI writers[4] as they coped with the details of the suicide attempt on January 28, 1977 of actor-comic Freddie Prinze (from which he subsequently died). The story first broke at 8:10 A.M.; a UPI "Urgent" interrupting the "Fourth World in Brief" report. For the next 12 hours, the story was carried as a regular item in the bulk of the "World in Brief" which followed. As you read the different versions, note how the writers emphasized new elements of the story to keep the reporting fresh and interesting. Also note that the wire service makes frequent typographical errors, which you will have to correct so that your newscast will make sense to the listener.

URGENT

(PRINZ)

(HOLLYWOOD)—ACTOR FREDDIE PRINZE, STAR OF THE "CHICO AND THE MAN" TELEVISION SHOW, WAS ADMITTED TO THE U-C-L-A MEDICAL CENTER IN LOS ANGELES EARLY TODAY SUFFERING A GUNSHOT WOUND TO THE HEAD. A SPOKESMAN AT U-C-L-A CONFIRMED THAT THE COMEDIAN WAS ADMITTED TO THE HOSPITAL BUT HAD NO WORD ON HIS CONDITION. CITY FIRE RESCUE OFFICERS WERE SUMMONED TO PRINZE'S WEST LOS ANGELES APARTMENT AT 3:57 A-M AND HE WAS RUSHED TO THE HOSPITAL THE 22-YEAR-OLD ACTOR, WHO PLAYS A MEXICAN-AMERICAN MECHANIC ON THE HIT SHOW, WAS RECENTLY SUED FOR DIVORCE BY HIS WIFE OF 15 MONTHS, KATHY ELAINE. THE COUPLE HAS A SON, FREDDIE.

UPI 01-28 08:10 AES

FIFTH-WORLD IN BRIEF

(LOS ANGELES)—ACTOR COMEDIAN FREDDIE PRINZE IS LISTED IN CRITICAL CONDITION AT THE U-C-L-A MEDICAL CENTER AFTER SUFFERING A GUNSHOT WOUND IN THE HEAD BEFORE DAWN TODAY. PRINZE WAS FOUND IN THE APARTMENT WHERE HE HAS BEEN LIVING SINCE HIS WIFE SUED FOR DIVORCE LAST YEAR. IT HASN'T BEEN DETERMINED IF THE GUNSHOT WAS SELF-INFLICTED. PRINZ IS THE STAR OF THE "CHICO AND THE MAN" T-V PROGRAM.

-28-

SIXTH WORLD IN BRIEF

(HOLLYWOOD)—SPOKESMEN AT U-C-L-A MEDICAL CENTER SAY ACTOR FREDDIE PRINZE—"CHICO" ON THE HIT T-V SERIES "CHICO AND THE MAN"—IS IN SERIOUS TO CRITICAL CONDITION AND A NEUROSURGEON HAS BEEN CALLED TO THE HOSPITAL FOR EMERGENCY SURGERY. PARA-

[4] Used by permission of UPI.

MEDICS SAY PRINZE WAS FOUND WITH A BULLET WOUND IN HIS HEAD
EARLY THIS MORNING. POLICE ARE CALLING IT A POSSIBLE SUICIDE AT-
TEMPT.
   -28-

EIGHTH WORLD IN BRIEF

(HOLLYWOOD)—COMEDIAN FREDDIE PRINZE IS HOSPITALIZED AT
U-C-L-A CENTER IN CRITICAL CONDITION WITH A BULLET WOUND IN THE
HEAD. THE 22-YEAR-OLD STAR OF "CHICO AND THE MAN" TRIED TO
COMMIT SUICIDE THIS MORNING . . . IN FRONT OF HIS BUSINESS MAN-
AGER . . . AFTER PHONING HIS PARENTS AND HIS ESTRANGED WIFE TO
TELL THEM HE WAS PLANNING ON TAKING HIS LIFE

PRINZE APPARENTLY WAS DESPONDENT OVER HIS RECENT DIVORCE
AND AN APPEARANCE IN COURT NEXT MONTH ON CHARGES OF DRIVING
UNDER THE INFLUENCE OF DRUGS. A NOTE WAS FOUND IN HIS WILSHIRE
BOULEVARD APARTMENT NEAR BEVERLY HILLS. IT READ—"I CAN'T
TAKE IT ANY LONGER."
28-

NINTH WORLD IN BRIEF

(HOLLYWOOD)—ACTOR FREDIE PRINZE IS IN CRITICAL CONDITION AT
U-C-L-A MEDICAL CENTER IN LOS ANGELES AFTER SHOOTING HIMSELF IN
THE HEAD. THE 22-YEAR-OLD STAR OF THE T-V SHOW "CHICO AND THE
MAN" WAS SAID TO BE DESPONDENT OVER HIS RECENT DIVORCE FROM
HIS WIFE OF 15 MONTHS. HE HAD BEEN TALKING THROUGH THE NIGHT
WITH VARIOUS FRIENDS ON THE TELEPHONE AND ASSOCIATES VISITED
HIM IN HIS LUXURY HOLLYWOOD APARTMENT.

TENTH WORLD IN BRIEF

(HOLLYWOOD) ONE OF AMERICA'S T-V FAVORITES LIES CRITICALLY
WOUNDED TODAY IN A LOS ANGELES HOSPITAL—TWO BULLET HOLES IN
HIS HEAD. ACTOR FREDDIE PRINZE SHOT HIMSELF IN THE TEMPLE AT 4
O'CLOCK THIS MORNING IN FRONT OF HIS HORRIFIED BUSINESS MAN-
AGER, MARVIN SNYDER. A POLICE OFFICER SAID THE BULLET WENT IN
ONE SIDE OF HIS HEAD AND OUT THE OTHER. HE WAS RUSHED TO U-C-L-A
MEDICAL CENTER, WHERE NEUROSURGEONS WENT INTO CONSULTATION
ON HIS CONDITION.

ELEVENTH WORLD IN BRIEF

(LOS ANGELES)—COMEDIAN FREDDIE PRINZE—DESPONDENT OVER A RECENT DIVORCE ACTION FILED BY HIS WIFE—TRIED TO COMMIT SUICIDE TODAY. THE 22-YEAR-OLD STAR OF "CHICO AND THE MAN" IS REPORTED NEAR DEATH AT U-C-L-A MEDICAL CENTER WITH A BULLET WOUND IN HIS HEAD.

TWELFTH WORLD IN BRIEF

(LOS ANGELES)—NEUROSURGEONS FOUGHT FOR TWO HOURS TO SAVE THE LIFE OF FREDDIE PRINZE—STAR OF T-V'S "CHICO AND THE MAN." THE 22-YEAR-OLD PRINZE—DESPONDENT OVER A DIVORCE ACTION BY HIS WIFE—SHOT HIMSELF IN THE HEAD THIS MORNING. HE'S HOSPITALIZED IN LOS ANGELES . . . WHERE DOCTORS SAY HE IS IN CRITICAL CONDITION.

THIRTEENTH WORLD IN BRIEF

-28-

(HOLLYWOOD)—COMEDIAN AND T-V STAR FREDDIE PRINZE IS REPORTED NEAR DEATH AFTER FIRING A BULLET THROUGH HIS BRAIN IN AN APPARENT SUICIDE ATTEMPT AT HIS HOLLYWOOD, CALIFORNIA, HOME THIS MORNING. NEUROSURGEONS AT U-C-L-A MEDICAL CENTER OPERATED FOR TWO HOURS IN AN EFFORT TO SAVE THE LIFE OF THE 22-YEAR-OLD STAR OF T-V'S "CHICO AND THE MAN." PRINZE . . . TROUBLED BY A RECENT DIVORCE AND AN IMPENDING TRIAL ON DRUG RELATED CHARGES . . . LEFT A NOTE DECLARING "I CAN'T TAKE IT ANY LONGER."

FOURTEENTH WORLD IN BRIEF

TELEVISION STAR FREDDIE PRINZE IS STILL CLINGING TO LIFE IN A LOS ANGELES HOSPITAL AFTER PUTTING A BULLET THROUGH HIS HEAD IN A FIT OF DESPONDENCY OVER A BROKEN MARRIAGE. DOCTORS AT U-C-L-A MEDICAL CENTER OPERATED FOR TWO HOURS IN AN EFFORT TO SAVE THE LIFE OF THE YOUNG COMEDIAN . . . STAR OF T-V'S "CHICO AND THE MAN."

FIFTEENTH WORLD IN BRIEF

(HOLLYWOOD)—IT IS UNCERTAIN AT THIS HOUR WHETHER THE STAR OF TELEVISION'S "CHICO AND THE MAN," FREDDIE PRINZE, WILL SUR-

VIVE A SUICIDE ATTEMPT. DOCTORS AT THE U-C-L-A MEDICAL CENTER PERFORMED TWO HOURS OF SURGERY AFTER THE 22-YEAR-OLD COMEDIAN PUT A BULLET THROUGH HIS HEAD EARLY THIS MORNING.

SIXTEENTH WORLD IN BRIEF

-28-

(LOS ANGELES)—THE STAR OF "CHICO AND THE MAN"—FREDDY PRINZE—IS REPORTED STILL ALIVE BUT IN CRITICAL CONDITION IN A LOS ANGELES HOSPITAL. PRINZE SHOT HIMSELF IN THE HEAD THIS MORNING BEFORE THE HORRIFIED EYES OF HIS BUSINESS MANAGER. HE WAS REPORTED DESPONDANT OVER A PENDING DIVORCE. THE HOSPITAL SAYS HE TOLERATED EMERGENCY SURGERY WELL . . . BUT IT CAN'T MAKE PREDICTIONS ABOUT HIS CHANCES OF SURVIVAL.

NINETEENTH WORLD IN BRIEF

(HOLLYWOOD)—COMEDIAN FREDDIE PRINZE—STAR OF TELEVISION'S "CHICO AND THE MAN"—IS BARELY CLINGING TO LIFE AFTER A FRIDAY MORNING SUICIDE ATTEMPT. A BULLET THROUGH THE HEAD REQUIRED TWO HOURS OF SURGERY IN A WEST LOS ANGELES HOSPITAL.

The "advance" label goes on any stories which can be moved early but should not be broadcast before a certain time. There are three types of advances. Some give the exact time of release: FOR AUTOMATIC RELEASE AT 11 A.M. CDT. Others are labeled FOR RELEASE EXPECTED ABOUT 11 A.M. CDT. The third type says FOR RELEASE EXPECTED SHORTLY. The latter two cannot be used until the wire sends down a release order: RELEASE X127 COLUMBIA ELECTION.

Although the wire services send down stories in specific order, it is left to you to use any portion, in any manner you wish. You have complete freedom to rewrite every wire you desire.

There is only one instance when you have no choice but to obey the wire services. That is the MANDATORY KILL. This order means just that. A news department's failure to kill a story at the request of the wire service could mean being dropped as a client in the case of UPI or as a member of AP. The wire service when it sends a KILL order has good reason; possible libel, or national security may be at stake, or the entire story may be false.

OTHER WIRE SERVICES

In addition to UPI and AP, the more ambitious news operation will subscribe to the other news wire services available. Although these are written primarily for newspapers, and therefore must be rewritten for broadcast, they provide additional excellent coverage and reports of events that the local station cannot cover itself. Included in this group of supplementary wire services are: The New York Times Service, The Copley News Service, the Dow Jones Business Wire, etc. In some areas, like Los Angeles, it is possible to subscribe to a service which specializes in coverage of city news.

ADDITIONAL NEWS SOURCES

Newsrooms should not limit their outside news sources to the national wires. They should also subscribe to the various magazines, periodicals and other publications which cover news events. Although many of these publications will not dwell on hard news, their feature style approach may give a tip-off for local features and ideas.

It goes without saying that each local newsroom should subscribe to every local newspaper within its broadcast area and at least one of the state's major newspapers which should be read religiously for feature items, upcoming news stories, etc. When an item is noted, it should be clipped, dated, and filed for future reference.[5]

While a good portion of the daily news diet can be dredged from the above sources, the hard, local news must be obtained from local sources—the police department, the mayor, the city manager, the city planner, the state police, etc.

Since the national services do not ordinarily cover local news, unless it takes on national importance, it is left to the local reporter to present the details of local developments.

It would be a meaningless waste of time to give a list of all possible sources for local news; some are rather obvious even to the public and some vary from community to community.[6]

For the beginning reporter, suffice to say that the most important thing to learn is which one of your various sources will have the desired information about a particular event. This knowledge cannot be spelled out for you; it takes a period of time in your community to know who is the "best guy to phone." It takes time and experience to find out that the secretary in the mayor's office is a better news source than the mayor himself. Or that through some quirk of local government, the city planner knows more about the workings of the public works department than anyone else.

The best technique for finding out the strange workings of your local news sources is to develop a regular routine of stopping by and seeing the sources.

[5] A "future file" is nothing more than a perpetual calendar consisting of 31 envelopes numbered 1–31 to correspond to the days of the month. The actual month is ignored. Thus your 15 file might contain information for events on the 15th of November, June, July, etc. Each day the file is checked to keep abreast of what events are coming up.

[6] A partial list of local sources might include: police department, mayor's office, city planner's office, local chamber of commerce, various municipal offices commissions, county clerk's office, local political organizations, local civic and community organizations, local school district office, etc.

Get to know them, and let them know you. After a while they will come to expect your visits and will begin to give you information.

It is impossible to offer specific directions on the methods of attracting and cultivating trustworthy news sources. Developing such a relationship demands the utmost in empathic communication skills while dealing with an infinite variety of people. Finding someone ''on the inside'' of a story who trusts you enough to reveal potentially harmful information takes time, commitment and a personality which encourages openness and honesty. These traits cannot be taught or precisely explained. The ability to handle news sources successfully can only be gained through the hard experience of trial and error as you strive to become a competent professional journalist. But one word of warning, don't ever start your visit by saying ''What's new?'' That's the fastest way to ruin a good source. When you go in, try and have some specific bit of information that you need. A direct question can often lead into a general discussion which might give you additional information.

Most reporters make the serious mistake of relying on well-established organizations for news and information. Spokespersons for business, government agencies, unions, and similar groups are media wise. They are usually willing to help reporters, are available for news conferences, and can be counted on to deliver a useful news item. These ''establishment'' figures, expert at media manipulation, provide a steady supply of quotes and interviews but total reliance on such sources can lead to a subtly biased viewpoint in your reporting.

Instead of seeking the obvious spokesperson for a story, look for the viewpoint normally ignored by other reporters. Often this will lead to an exclusive angle on a particular development or, at the least, more balanced coverage.

A good example of this problem is the coverage of labor strikes. The majority of reports consist of interviews with industry and labor leaders. The workers themselves are blurred faces in the background. Instead of going to the usual sources, a resourceful reporter might do a story from the viewpoint of the average worker, thus giving a different perspective to the occurrence. The same approach can be applied to other situations. For example, instead of the normal report on a murder with the predictable statements from the police, why not a story from a suspect's frame of reference?

A successful reporter cultivates sources both inside and outside the normal social organizations. Everyone should be regarded as a potential supplier of news. Only by developing a sensitivity to the trivial event, can a reporter hope to completely report the news of a community.

Not only is society divided in terms of those inside and outside the power structure, but it is also divided vertically by class and social position. Since you will be a professional member of the middle-class, you will spend most of your news-gathering time with others in your class or higher on the social ladder.

Those in the upper ranks of our society attempt to attract your professional attention by their offers of free meals, drinks, and junkets. It is difficult to resist such ''freebies.'' It is not my intention to argue the morality of such relationships, but you should make a serious effort to strike a balance in your reporting duties.

There are other groups in our culture; groups who cannot afford to buy you a steak dinner or drinks, nor offer slickly packaged media presentations to use in preparing your stories. Too often, the very groups who have trouble gaining access to news programs are the ones whose plight is the most demanding. As a reporter, it is your obligation to make yourself available to *all* groups in a community no matter how much you may disagree with their positions. If you can establish a sense of trust with those representing alternative viewpoints, you will be able to prepare a more balanced news report, that is an essential goal for a professional journalist.

After you have established yourself with your sources, it is possible to maintain a daily liaison with them by telephone if a busy schedule does not permit in-person chats. The telephone is an important tool. It saves time, and will on many occasions get you in where a personal appearance will fail. For some reason telephone calls take priority over face-to-face interviews.

As you are trying to track down a source by telephone, it's a good idea to keep an alphabetical index of all phone numbers of sources you run into during the day. You should list these under the names of their organizations or areas of interest. You should also include a brief note describing what type of information the source can supply so that others can also use your file and so that you can reach a source more efficiently in the future.

One overlooked source of potential features are the stacks of free public relations handouts, audio tapes, etc. These "news releases," while often only seeking free publicity, very often can lead to solid features with important news value.

Many veteran reporters refuse to read public relations material they receive through the mail, dismissing it out-of-hand as "non-news." This is a grave error. While it is true that much of the publicity material received by a news department is of questionable news value, very often a release will lend itself to feature treatment or will develop into a news story with further investigation.

The most valuable news releases are those that announce some future event such as the opening of a new school, bridge, department store, etc. These should be noted and placed in the future file for possible coverage on the day of the event.

Often radio stations will receive free audio tapes distributed by a public relations organization on behalf of its client such as the United Nations, magazines such as *Sports Illustrated,* various senators and congressmen, etc. These tapes, if run in their entirety, would constitute nothing more than a subtle advertisement for the client. But, it is your privilege to edit the tape in any manner you wish and use only those parts you consider of news value. It should also be noted that you are required to name the source when this information could have a bearing on the item's credibility or objectivity.

For example, your station might receive a tape from a sports magazine

featuring one of its staff interviewing a noted baseball player. Included prominently on the tape in a number of spots is the magazine's name. You are free to
edit the tape in such a manner as to leave only the player's comments, relegating
the magazine interviewer and the name of the publication to the wastebasket.

But if you received a tape featuring a statement from General Motors against
a possible strike by auto workers, it is essential that you name GM as your source
to alert your audience to any possible bias in the tape.

Even obvious publicity pieces can be used by a creative writer who can
turn a pompous sounding release into an off-beat, humorous report. For example, a few years ago a state highway commission kicked off a campaign to choose
the most picturesque highway structure in the state and asked the public to vote
for their favorite bridge, viaduct or sign-post.

This was obviously a publicity campaign, but a clever writer took the hand-
out and used it as the basis for a tongue-in-cheek, "man-in-the-street" interview
which was included in one of the evening newscasts. True, it wasn't "hard"
news of vital importance, but it was an entertaining comment on the country's
desire to honor almost everything.

Once, with a few spare moments, I cast a cynical eye at America's penchant for holidays honoring almost everything. I came up with a two-minute
feature spelling out in great detail the value of the annual "Buzzard Day" cele-
bration in Hinkley, Ohio, the ". . . not to be forgotten joys of National Mother-
in-Law Day," and other festivals that dot our calendar. A bit of whimsy to be
sure, but it went a long way towards livening up a dull news day.

A good writer can find a feature or a news angle in just about anything,
and it is this type of writing that helps make for a successful news production.

THE TELEPHONE INTERVIEW

I have already discussed the importance of the telephone as an efficient
method of getting in touch with news sources. But the telephone serves another
important function in radio news. It provides an endless supply of recorded interviews and "actualities" which, when combined with effective writing, make
the news exciting and informative.

There are two basic types of telephone recordings used in radio news: the
"beeper" and the "actuality." The former refers to an interview or statement
by some person in the news, while the latter consists of those reports which
include actual sounds from the event.

Telephone interviews may make up the lion's share of many news operations' daily programs. The telephone allows a small staff to get in contact with
widely separated news sources that otherwise could not be reached.

The procedure for conducting a beeper interview with a subject is me-
chanically simple. All that is needed is a tape recorder, a signaling device (the
"beeper") provided by the telephone company and the telephone. The three

units are wired together to allow the tape recorder to record both sides of the conversation directly from the telephone circuitry, thereby reducing background noise and interference. To help improve the quality of recordings, it is advisable to have the telephone equipped with a button which will shut off the newsroom side of the conversation to completely cut out extraneous noise. The telephone company for a slight charge will make all the necessary connections.

Now that you have the tape recorder all set up, what next? To the novice reporter, interviewing is probably the hardest skill to master. It is something that is learned through years of experience requiring a growing awareness of handling people and getting them to comment on things they may feel reluctant to discuss.

While it is impossible to give specific rules for conducting a telephone beeper interview, there are certain tricks-of-the-trade that may work for you.

1. You must identify yourself: "This is Bob Jones of KCHO news," and tell your subject why you are calling: "I am phoning to get your reaction to the governor's move to increase the property tax. . . ."
2. You should also tell your subject that you are recording the interview. If he balks, explain that it is better for *him* since there will be no chance of mis-quoting or misinterpreting his statements. If he refuses, turn off the recorder and continue interviewing while taking notes.
3. If the subject is hesitant about stating his views on a particular subject, you might point out that you are only trying to get his side of the controversy. "We already have the views of your opponent . . . and we would like to present a balanced picture. . . ."
4. If he still refuses, you might ask him why he refuses to comment. His an-swer might make an interesting story in itself.
5. If you are asking someone for details about an incident and he refuses to help, you could point out that you already have the information from another source but you would like his version to clear up any possible confusion.
6. If the subject agrees to be interviewed, then comes the next hurdle: What do you ask? The best technique is to ask those kinds of questions that require more than a yes or no answer. Ask "How do you feel about . . . ?" or "Do you agree with . . . ?" or "If the bill passes, what do you think will be its effect?" These types of questions will elicit responses that will be more interesting and informative than so-called "closed-ended" questions.
7. If your subject answers yes or no to a direct question, you should immedi-ately ask why.
8. After you ask each question, push the "kill" button and wait through his entire answer, listening carefully to his comments; they will give you a lead as to what to ask next.
9. While the subject is answering your questions do not interject comments like "I see," "you're right," etc. They make it very difficult to edit the tape after the interview. Once the subject starts talking, that is your signal to remain quiet.

10. Keep the recorder running during the entire interview. You never know when the subject may say something of value.
11. If the subject says something you consider startling or unusual, *don't* ask his permission to use the comment. If you have already told him you are recording the interview, you already have his permission. Asking may raise doubts in his mind about the advisability of making this specific statement public.
12. Don't ever promise that you will allow the subject to preview your story and the edited tape.
13. At the end of the interview simply say you feel you have sufficient information, thank him for his cooperation, and hang up.

Quite often to get a subject to cooperate and willing to talk it is necessary to resort to every maneuver you can think of. For example, a few years ago there was a fire in a small Missouri town. First reports were confused but did include the name of one eyewitness. I contacted him by telephone, told him I would like to do an interview and this is the conversation which followed. My explanatory remarks are in brackets:

ME: I understand you saw the fire begin, is that true? [*trying to find out if he indeed saw what happened.*]

1. HIM: Well, yes, but I don't think what I have to say would contribute anything.

ME: Why not? [*Keep after him, once he hangs up, you're finished.*]

2. HIM: Well, I really didn't see that much.

ME: What did you see?

3. HIM: I'd rather not say.

ME: Why not?

4. HIM: The situation is very confused and I think I would only be adding to it.

ME: Well Mr. _____, I have had a number of reports on the fire and I am completely confused. Since you were an eyewitness I'm hoping that maybe you could help clear up the confusion. . . . [*asking for his help puts him in proper frame of mind.*]

5. HIM: Well, I really didn't see very much. Perhaps if you asked me some specific question, I might be able to help.

ME: Fine. Now when you looked out the window, what did you see?

6. HIM: I was working at my desk when I heard a loud explosion. I looked out the window and saw fire pouring out the windows. . . . [*Then followed a five-minute statement relating the details of the fire and explosion.*]

You will notice that I didn't give up. I kept the subject talking. If there is any cardinal principle in conducting an interview, it is *keep the subject talking.* If you are lucky sooner or later the subject will break down and tell you what you want to know. Obviously there will be those occasions when even this won't work. You will just have to learn when it is time to give up, a sixth sense that only comes with experience.

I now have an excellent five-minute description of the fire. But my editor tells me he can only use two minutes on the story so I am faced with the task of editing my interview. I review my notes and listen to the tape, noting the subject's statements and their approximate length. My notes might look like this:

1. HIM: I was working at my desk . . . :20
   ME: Did you see anyone getting out the front door?
2. HIM: . . . no one that I could see . . . :60
   ME: What was the nature of the fire?
3. HIM: . . . flash explosion . . . flared up . . . :75
   ME: Did you hear any cries from inside?
4. HIM: . . . didn't hear a thing . . . must've all died at once :45
   ME: We understand fire was set deliberately?
5. HIM: . . . don't know anything about it . . . . :25

Since I will need about 20 seconds to introduce the story, another 10 seconds to bridge between the various tape cuts, and another 10 seconds to wrap up the story, I can only use 1:20 worth of tape.

The first thing I can do to edit the tape is to drop all the questions. It is more important to air what the subject said rather than what I asked. In place of the questions, I can present additional information about the fire. I would also drop everything else that does not add needed news details.

Looking over the list of questions and answers, it is apparent that answers (3), (4), and (5) are of less news value and can be left out without damaging the impact of the story. That leaves questions (1) and (2).

With the tape editing out of the way, I must still put the two cuts together in the script, which might appear like this:

A flash fire . . . which police say was deliberately set . . . gutted the first floor tavern of the Randolph Hotel in Moberly an hour ago, killing 12 persons. So far no identification of the victims has been made.

An eyewitness . . . Frank Thomas . . . saw the blaze begin and described it as a flash explosion which flared up instantaneously:

ROLL TAPE: I was working at my desk. . . .

END TAPE: . . . flared up instantly. (:20)

Thomas says he didn't see anyone come out of the tavern after the fire started.

ROLL TAPE: No one got out alive. . . .

END TAPE: . . . just a massive wall of flames.(:60)

Police are presently questioning a suspect about the blaze. They say he voluntarily surrendered moments after the fire began.

You will notice in introducing the two tape inserts, I have purposely avoided mentioning that a tape is coming next. I have left out such phrases as:

In the interview you will hear. . . .

In a recorded statement. . .

In the following interview, Frank Thomas said. . . .

There is nothing wrong with phrases like these. But if the tape doesn't run because of mechanical problems, I will sound foolish having introduced it.

It is best to use "open-end" introductions to tape inserts whenever possible. This means writing the "intro" in such a fashion that will allow the story to still make sense to the listener if the tape doesn't run as planned. This will avoid embarrassment and explanations of what happened.

The most common technique in writing a tape "intro" is to summarize in a sentence or two what the tape says. But you should avoid the same phrasing as the insert. Look again at the above story and you can see how the script would make sense even without the tape. This should be your objective when writing introductions.

You should limit your beeper cuts to one minute or less; any longer and your listener's interest declines rapidly. Any comment, by anyone, can be edited by a skillful reporter into a number of short, dramatic cuts. It is more effective to edit a five-minute statement into three or four short cuts with bridge material between each one paraphrasing the speaker than to run the entire five minute remark.

This tightening process is the hallmark of a good news operation. It is the lazy reporter who allows a tape interview to run unedited.

Much of what is said is trivial and will cloud the newsworthy statements. It is possible to distill five minutes worth of comment into 30 seconds of rewritten material and make the speaker's comments take on significance and meaning which were hazy in the original.

THE ACTUALITY FEED

The second type of phone recording used in news work is the "actuality." Unlike the beeper, it is a portion of some event recorded in the field by a reporter and relayed via telephone to the newsroom or carried back and edited from the recorder.

The editing process for actualities is the same as for beepers except it is difficult to write open-end introductions since you are obviously replaying something which is already over.

Your introduction to an actuality should set the scene for listeners and alert them that a report "from the scene" is coming next. The intro should be brief and should not give away the details of the report:

ANCHORMAN: At city hall, the mayor has blasted a request to rezone the southern section of town as sought by General Electric . . . reporter Darran Leftwig reports. . . . (ROLL TAPE)

Actuality material or reports should not be used as time fillers or as a crutch. Some network affiliates, which record network actualities fed down the line via telephone during the day, often use them only because they can't think of anything else to fill the hourly newscast. Whether actualities are local or national, they should be included only when they add to the believability of the news.

There is one other type of recorded material available to radio news—the "voicer." This is different from the two previous types as it indicates that a reporter is giving a report from a remote location via telephone. Although it might include an actuality of the event, its major thrust is as a field report presenting up-to-the-minute details.

If your news department is fortunate enough to be able to afford large numbers of field reporters with complete freedom of movement and an unlimited travel budget, you will have your area adequately covered. But, if yours is a station and cannot afford correspondents, your regional and state coverage may be limited to wire service reports.

However, there is one solution—"news exchange." If you receive a wire story of an important news break in another city in your region and you can't afford to send a reporter or there isn't time, you might try phoning one of the local radio or television news stations in that city and requesting a voicer report from one of *their* reporters.

Usually, these stations are more than willing to cooperate and will furnish you with whatever stories you need. They do this because some day a big story may break in your area and they will be phoning you.

Telephoning distant stations for news coverage is an excellent way of adding variety to your newscasts. However, you should not use these reports indiscriminately. They should only be sought and used when they will add meaning and depth to the reports of the event.

Never hesitate to phone another station for a report. Simply ask for the news department and request that they supply you with a voicer about the story. Unless they are restricted by union regulations, they will usually supply you with a one or two minute story which you can record and later play back on your newscasts.

The easiest way to find out which stations are located in a particular area is to look up the city in the latest issue of *Broadcasting Yearbook* which will also include their telephone numbers.

4

Police, Crime and Criminal Law

AS YOU WILL QUICKLY find out, the major share of local news will come from the police station. If anything is covered adequately by a local station, it is police, crime news, and courtroom activity. This is so, not because the crime news is considered to be so important, but because in addition to having the details of robberies, murders, vandalism and the like, the police department is also the clearing house for almost all community activities. The police are the first to learn of auto accidents, attempted suicides, missing persons, rabid dogs, strikes, protest demonstrations, fires and many other events of great local interest.

If you're assigned the "cop shop," you will be given the task of covering the police beat which means checking the police department three or four times a day, visiting the scenes of the infrequent, important crimes that occur, and writing all the police reports worth mentioning.

But the reporting doesn't stop with the arrest, it continues through the entire judicial procedure; a complex, and often confusing labyrinth of legal procedures that must be understood before you can hope to grasp the significance of a particular court action or ruling.

It is beyond the scope of this book to present a full course in American jurisprudence. My purpose is merely to explain the workings of our legal system so you will be able to explain the various procedures to your audience if need be.

POLICE DEPARTMENT ORGANIZATION

Every town in the country has a police force. It may consist of one part-time officer who patrols at night and runs a grocery store by day. It may boast of an army of police officers that rivals the complexity of the armed forces. But whatever its size, the police have the obligation to protect society from those bent on breaking its laws. Police are legally empowered only to enforce the law—not to make laws.

What the police force does is public information and the public has the right to know about it, and you have the responsibility to report it. There is a continuing discussion between the bar and the press over your right to cover criminal activities, a subject I shall look at later in more detail.

It should be made perfectly clear that not all police news has to do with crime. The beginning reporter assigned to the police beat should be constantly on the look-out for human interest stories which pour in a steady stream across the pages of the police records.

Policemen, like other public servants, are political creatures. They are subject to pressures and graft. And news stories about police shakeups, promotions and demotions, graft, physical mistreatment of prisoners, poor jail conditions, etc. are also stories which must be given adequate coverage when they occur.

You must know the organization of the local police department if you are going to be able to find out necessary details about a particular event. While the structure may differ slightly from city to city, the average size police force usually has a well-established table of organization, which, once learned and understood, can make your job much easier.

At the top is always a chief of police, superintendent, commissioner or some other individual appointed by the city government in power. But whatever the title, the person holding the top job is a political appointee and thus may have little or nothing to say about general police policies. Their job is to present the proper image to the community. They "front" for the city administration which passes along its decisions through their office.

Under the chief is the captain; the true, day-to-day executive of the police department. In small communities, the chief may assume this responsibility. In large cities, each precinct station is commanded by a captain in quasi-military fashion. The lieutenants head up each of the different operating divisions, such as traffic, detective, and patrol. Sergeants perform the same function in the police department as their military counterpart. They are charged with carrying out orders from the top by directing the patrolmen under their command. Inspectors may have roving assignments to check up on the operations of the various stations or may perform the function of lieutenants; it is largely a matter of local terminology.

In larger cities the police force is divided up into separate divisions, squads, bureaus and departments with specific areas of responsibility. You will have officers who specialize in homicide, vice, traffic, arson, burglary, auto theft, fraud, etc. The larger the force, the more the specialization. Some forces rotate their personnel among the various divisions to provide them with a well-rounded knowledge. Others permanently assign a given area and their officers become experts in that particular illegal activity.

As a reporter it is essential that you get to know as many people in the police department as you can, so that you'll be able to quickly locate the right person when you need information on a story.

In addition to city police, you will probably also cover the sheriff's office, which is the police force for the unincorporated areas of a county. It enforces the law in those parts of the county which are not within city limits.

Ordinarily the sheriff's office is smaller than a city police department and its staff may not be as well trained. Historically, the office of sheriff is political—sheriffs are elected and often appoint deputies as political favors.

Finally, each state has its state police force. It may be called the Highway Patrol (California), the State Police (New York), or the Rangers (Texas). But whatever its title, the state police are primarily responsible for maintaining control of the state's highway system. In some states you also have a state bureau of criminal investigation which operates much like a city police detective bureau.

On the national level is the Federal Bureau of Investigation which is headquartered in Washington, D.C., and has regional offices throughout the country. The FBI is *not* a national police force. Its only function is to investigate federal crimes and to lend the services of its crime laboratories to local authorities in their investigations. The FBI acts as a national clearing house for police information: fingerprints, arrest records, evidence, etc.

The federal government also has other law enforcement officers with specific responsibilities not under the jurisdiction of other agencies. The Treasury Department agents, for example, specialize in investigating counterfeiting. The Secret Service is primarily charged with guarding the president; a job they take very seriously as you will find out if you ever have the opportunity to cover an event involving the chief executive or a presidential candidate.

THE COURTS SYSTEM

When a person is arrested and charged with a crime the responsibility of the police is complete. The suspect is taken immediately to jail and held pending arraignment.

In most states suspects can be held for up to 48 hours without formal charges. After that they must either be released or formally accused of committing a crime. If formal charges are not brought, suspects can file for a writ of *habeas corpus* and be freed. Such a writ means the police have failed to prove they have grounds to hold them.

Assuming there is a formal charge filed, there are a number of specific steps which must then be followed. The person is "booked" (his name is written in the police record book along with a formal charge) and brought before a judge for arraignment. The judge uses this occasion to inform the defendant of the charges, hear a plea, and assure proper representation by a defense lawyer.

What happens next depends on the nature of the charge.[1] If it is a mis-

---

[1] Generally, a misdemeanor is a crime punishable by a sentence of one year or *less* in the county jail. A felony is punishable by one year or more in the state prison or penitentiary. The difference between the two is determined strictly by the length of sentence, which may be set at the judge's discretion in

demeanor, the judge can set the case for trial, or the defendant may plead guilty and receive sentence on the spot, the usual practice in traffic courts.

If the charge is a felony, the judge at the arraignment may not be the same judge who will ultimately hear the case since felonies are tried in superior courts while most initial arraignments are heard in municipal courts. Municipal courts do not have jurisdiction for the more serious violations of state law.

The municipal judge arraigns the suspect and schedules a preliminary hearing. This hearing, somewhat informal in nature, determines whether there are reasonable grounds for scheduling a regular trial. Should it be determined that the charge is unfounded, the defendant is released. Remember though, being discharged at this point does not give the suspect the protection of the double jeopardy statutes. He may be arrested again if new evidence is uncovered.

If the preliminary hearing judge decides there is sufficient grounds, the accused is "bound over" to the grand jury, which means he remains in jail or free on bond until the grand jury acts on the case.

The grand jury normally conducts a very one-sided hearing, listening to only the state's case to determine whether the case is strong enough to go to trial. The grand jury hearing is not a trial because there is usually no opportunity for the defendant to present a case. In fact, the defendant is often not even allowed to attend the hearings.[2]

The hearing, conducted under great secrecy and closed to the press, is completed when the jury members return a "true bill"—the indictment or the final list of charges against the suspect. The indictment may merely repeat the original charge filed by the police or it may have increased the number of charges, or, in some instances, reduced the number or severity of charges.

Of course, the grand jury may refuse to indict which means the suspect is released. But, as in the preliminary hearing, he may be arrested if new evidence is discovered.

Grand juries also have independent investigative powers aside from handing down indictments. A grand jury may investigate any problem it feels may possibly involve criminal activity or neglect. If criminal activity is uncovered, the grand jury will order the county district attorney's office to prepare formal charges, the suspects will be arrested and go through the entire arraignment procedure.

But if an indictment is returned, defendants are called before the bench and go through a formal arraignment procedure where they are read the list of charges filed by the grand jury. Defendants are also required to enter a plea at this hearing. If they plead guilty, the judge may hand down sentence or may take the matter under advisement and set a later date for sentencing. If the accused pleads not guilty, the case is set for trial.

---

many instances. A person convicted of a felony must serve a sentence in a state prison, and likewise, a person found guilty of a misdemeanor must serve a term in the county jail. *Ballentine Law Dictionary* (1969) 3rd Edition.

[2] If it desires, the grand jury may hear the defendant if it feels there is a possibility that testimony might explain the evidence. However, the appearance of a defendant is strictly at the convenience of the grand jury.

In some states and in the federal courts, defendants are permitted to enter a plea of *nolo contendere*—no contest. This action simply means that the defendant has no defense to the charge, and is willing to accept the punishment of the court. It is not equivalent to a guilty plea; the defendant has not said he is guilty of any wrong doing, he just admits he has no defense. This legal hair-splitting is important because it means if other court action in the case is begun, there is no prior record of admission of guilt.

In the federal court system, the defendant is arraigned during the preliminary hearing, the two steps being combined into one.

PRE-TRIAL MOTIONS AND OTHER MANEUVERS

Once the defendant had been legally informed of the charges, he and his attorney will begin preparing for the trial. Some of this preparation may include the filing of various defense pre-trial motions designed to challenge the validity of the state's case, or get the trial moved to another area or different judge.

Motion to Delay seeks to have the trial date postponed in the hopes that public emotion may subside, or to give time for more adequate preparation, gathering of evidence, etc.

Motion to Quash the Indictment questions the validity of the indictment on the grounds of insufficient evidence, unconstitutional procedures, etc. If the judge rules in favor of the defense, he will void the indictment. However, this does not bar the state from seeking another indictment and further prosecution.

Motion for a Bill of Particulars seeks more detailed information about the charges in the indictment. If the motion is successful, the state is forced to reveal more about how it plans to prosecute the case.

Motion for a Change of Venue is a move on the part of the defense to have the case moved to another court because the attorney may feel the trial judge is prejudiced or that it would be impossible to gather an impartial jury. If the judge supports the motion, the case is transferred to another court in a different part of the state, or, in the case of a federal trial, it may be moved to another state.

Motion to Suppress Evidence is filed to prohibit the use of certain evidence or testimony that the defense feels was gathered by unconstitutional methods. Included would be evidence gathered by illegal search and seizure, entrapment, illegal wiretapping, improper arrest procedures, etc. A ruling in favor of the defense simply means that this material is inadmissable and the case might then be challenged on grounds of insufficient evidence and possibly dismissed.

Motion of Nolle Prosequi is the one important motion which can be filed by the state. It means that the state does not wish to prosecute. It is filed when the prosecution becomes convinced that the defendent is innocent.

THE TRIAL

As we know, the accused is entitled to a jury trial. If he waives that right, his case will be heard before the judge who will hear both sides, determine guilt and pass sentence. If a jury trial is held, the jury alone determines guilt or innocence on the basis of testimony and evidence presented during the trial. In some states, it is also the jury which decides the punishment, and in others it is the judge's responsibility to fix penalty.

The selection of the jury, usually a routine procedure, can be interesting and newsworthy if the two sides decide to hotly contest the seating of the various jurors. Normally a number of citizens are called for jury duty. This jury panel is the pool from which the 12 members of the trial jury will finally be chosen. Some states have 16 persons sitting as the jury, the four extra in case one of the 12 gets ill and must be excused.

In selecting the jury the opposing attorneys will question each prospective juror until the panel is full. Each side is looking for people who it feels will render a fair verdict; in other words, be favorably disposed towards its side. Each side is entitled to a certain limited number of "peremptory challenges." These allow the dismissal of a juror for any reason whatever. Potential jurors may also be refused by "challenging for cause." This type of objection is not limited in number and seeks dismissal on grounds such as prejudice, friendships with either side, etc.

Once the jury is selected and sworn in, the trial begins. Lawyers for both sides give their opening statements in which they outline to the court what they will attempt to prove. Then the prosecution presents its case after which the defense is permitted to present its counter-evidence.

When the defense rests its case, the state has the opportunity for rebuttal—the calling back of previous state witnesses. The defense does not have this right.

After this step, both sides present their summations. This is probably the emotional peak of the trial as both sides pull out all the stops. First the prosecution pictures the defendant as the worst type of criminal and then the defense presents him as a poor soul who wouldn't harm a fly.

After the dramatics, the judge charges the jury, telling them what legal principles are involved in the case, what verdict they can return and what the possible penalties may be.

If the jury returns a verdict of not guilty (when you report a verdict on radio always write it in terms of "innocent" or "guilty," the word *not* may be missed by your audience), that is the end of the case. If the jury cannot reach a verdict, the judge declares a hung jury and orders a new trial before a new jury. If the verdict is guilty, the judge may pass sentence then or at a later date.

A guilty verdict automatically prompts the defense to announce it will seek an appeal. The judge, delaying sentence, gives the defense a specific number of days, usually 30, within which to file a motion for a retrial.

The defense motion consists of arguments to support a new trial on the grounds that legal and procedural errors in the original trial nullify the verdict. If the judge grants the motion, the verdict is set aside and a new hearing is scheduled before a different judge and jury. If the motion is overruled, sentencing takes place and the prisoner pays the penalty as proscribed by law.

In some states the law specifically says what sentence will be handed down for certain crimes. The law may say "manslaughter conviction—eight years." In those cases, the judge is obligated to impose that sentence. On the other hand, the law may call for a "sentence of one to ten years." In that case, the judge may hand down a sentence of from one to ten years depending on future conduct of the prisoner in prison, or for any period within that range. During the prison term, the felon will become eligible for parole after a specified period of time.

The passing of sentence does not end the appeal procedure which may be carried on as long as the prisoner's patience and funds hold out. These appeals may delay, or possibly prevent entirely, imprisonment. The appeal is filed within a specified period of time with the next highest court—state supreme court, federal circuit court, or the U.S. Supreme Court, depending on the original court of jurisdiction.

At any point in the appeals procedure, a higher court may reverse the lower court's decision and order a new trial, or it may simply reverse the decision and order the defendent freed.

It should be pointed out that recent court rulings have modified the concept of double jeopardy. The courts have ruled that if a defendant is found innocent in a *state* court of some offense, he may be tried in a *federal* court if there was a violation of federal law involved. Conversely, if a person is tried and acquitted of a federal crime, they may be charged and brought to trial under a state statute.

It should be obvious that the trial system is a complex and confusing process. It is your responsibility when reporting on court activities, to explain the importance of these various procedures to the listener who is probably not familiar with the various intricacies of the judicial system.

FAIR TRIAL VS. FREE PRESS

News coverage of police activity and trials raises the crucial problem of a free press versus a fair trial. Can a defendant get a fair trial while the press is exercising its constitutional freedom to editorially comment on the crime, the trial and to urge specific verdicts?

Lawyers and journalists tend to see the problem at its two extremes: At one end of the spectrum are the secret trials of dictatorships where public scrutiny is completely denied. At the other extreme is "trial by media." Each step of the procedure is reported and commented on by the media to the point where it is impossible to tell if the verdict was the result of evidence introduced in court or public opinion stirred up by the media.

In a 1976 landmark First Amendment decision, the U.S. Supreme Court unanimously curtailed the power of judges to control news coverage of public trials.

The case arose when a Nebraska judge had ordered a total media blackout regarding a murder case because he feared the effect on jurors. The Supreme Court held that the Nebraska courts had no right to tell the press what it could publish or broadcast during the case, but at the same time refused to absolutely prohibit "gag orders." This leaves the way open for direct restraints on the press if extraordinary circumstances warrant such action.

Also left for future consideration was the related issue of whether a judge could gag the press by barring the public from the courtroom and sealing the trial records.

Chief Justice Warren Burger made it clear the Court would not decide between the First and Sixth Admendments: a free press vs. fair trial. He said the writers of the Constitution did not set one Amendment above the other and "it is not for us to rewrite the Constitution."

Even though the ruling does not clearly define the power of the press to cover trials, it does re-affirm the right of the public to know about the workings of the criminal justice system.

How far may society go to limit news reports to guarantee a fair trial is a question which will continue to plague journalists and lawyers alike. It is unlikely a satisfactory answer will be found; however, there are guidelines which would assist both the press and the courts.

The Minnesota Fair-Trial Press Council prepared a list of such policies that, if followed by police and honored by reporters, may go a long way to solving the controversy:

The following information generally *should* be made public at, or immediately following, the time of arrest:
1. The accused's name, age, residence, employment, marital status, and similar background information.
2. The substance or text of the charge, such as is, or would be contained in a complaint, indictment or information.
3. The identity of the investigating and arresting agency and the length of the investigation.
4. The circumstances immediately surrounding an arrest, including the time and place of arrest, resistance, pursuit, possession and use of weapons, and a description of items at the time of arrest.

The following information generally *should not* be made public at, or immediately after, the time of arrest:
1. Statements as to the character or reputation of an accused person.
2. Existence or contents of any confession, admission or statement given by the accused, or a refusal to make a statement.
3. Performance of results of tests, or the refusal of an accused to take such a test.
4. Expected content of testimony, or credibility of prospective witnesses.
5. Possibility of a plea of guilty to the offense charged or to a lesser offense, or other disposition.
6. Other statements relating to the merits, evidence, argument, opinions or theories of the case.

5

Reporting the Disaster, Civil Disturbance and Terrorist Story

WHILE THE MAJOR SHARE of news coverage is routine—dealing with the activities of various governmental agencies, pronouncements from politicians, and the other items that comprise the bulk of the daily news diet—occasionally the reporter is confronted with covering an event that transcends the normal: the disaster.

Giving the public the information it must have about these types of events is a critical and important process. If it is handled poorly, it can create concern, panic, and even widespread havoc.

It is impossible to give you a number of specific rules to follow when you are sent to cover a wide-ranging, fast-breaking news story. I can only suggest some general guidelines that may keep you from making serious mistakes in judgment and coverage.

It is hoped that you never have to cover a disaster. But sooner or later you will have to, and you will probably find these occasions among the most exciting and interesting moments of your career.

When you are sent to report on such a story, you should be well aware of your responsibilities to both the participants in the event and to your audience. You must be aware that how you handle yourself and your reports can affect the situation; a poor job of reporting may cause more damage than the event itself.

For one thing, you must know when to call an event a disaster, and when not to. In other words, you should know when not to make your report of a particular news event so alarming and shocking that your story itself adds to the general panic.

A traffic accident is a disaster in a sense, especially to those involved. A child trapped at the bottom of a well is a disaster to the victim and his family. A fire that kills 10 persons is a disaster to them. But in the callous world of news reporting, none of these, or similar incidents, are worthy of the general term *disaster*.

You must realize that such things happen a dozen times a day. An event becomes a disaster in the news sense when the magnitude of the death and destruction reaches gigantic proportions. For example, the crash of a private plane which kills three persons is not a disaster. The crash of a passenger plane killing 100 or more is a disaster and can rightly be called so.

These events are dramatic, exciting, and full of human emotions that go beyond the people closely involved in the event. It is this last criterion that makes these stories stand above the run-of-the-mill item. They are so complex that the reporter does not know where to begin. There are so many parts of an overall news story breaking at once that it is difficult to decide what to do first.

Chances are that the great majority of disaster stories you are called upon to report will be provided by the wire services. You are then faced with the problem of reporting something on the basis of information provided by sources outside your immediate area, sources you cannot contact for more facts. The only thing you can do when faced with this problem is to rely on the judgment of the wire services and make sure that you play up the local angle whenever possible.

If the disaster is of major dimensions, there is usually a casuality list circulated. Scan the list looking for local names which you would include in your lead, as in the following example taken from an item describing a plane crash in Chicago:

> Four local residents are among the 112 victims of that crash of a Boeing 747 jet passenger plane 15 miles south of Chicago.
> Listed as killed in the crash were: 43-year old Robert Jennings, his wife Edith. . . .

Occasionally, however, the disaster will occur within your broadcast service area and you will be called upon to prepare reports from first-hand observations. The easiest way to describe what you *should* and *should not* do is to create a disaster situation and trace it from the first reports, through the height of the incident, and finally to the follow-up stories.

A fire breaks out in a local hotel in the early morning hours. By the time firemen arrive on the scene, the blaze is completely out of control.

For some strange reason disasters seem to always occur in the small hours of the morning and you are rousted from a sound sleep and ordered to report to the scene to cover the story as it develops. Because of the urgency of the situation, it is impossible to round up an entire news crew, give them a complete briefing and send every available reporter to the scene. You are on your own.

The first thing to remember is to stay calm and go about the process of gathering as much factual information as you can. This process should begin even as you approach the scene. Make mental notes on what you see: How many fire trucks? How high are the flames leaping? What part of the building seems to be burning the fiercest? What kind of crowd controls are in effect? Any ambulances on the site?

Look for the fire chief. Wait until he seems to have a few spare seconds and ask some short, direct questions: Are all the guests out of the hotel? Any left inside? Any fatalities? Is the fire under control? Any idea how it started? Is there danger of it spreading?

After talking to the chief, walk around a little and see what is going on: Are nearby stores being evacuated? Any eyewitnesses see fire start? Do any of the evacuees have a statement? How were they warned of the fire? Were they able to rescue any personal goods?

As soon as you have gathered enough of the basic facts, get to a telephone. What you have learned is useless unless you can relay that information to your newsroom. But be careful what you tell them. Don't pass along rumors or unconfirmed information. If you have unconfirmed facts that you feel may later be proven, make sure thay they are labeled as speculation—not truth. For example:

> A four alarm fire is raging out of control in the Downtown Hotel at this hour. *It is not yet known* if there have been any fatalities. The fire chief says the blaze should be under control within the hour and he sees no threat to adjoining buildings. Police investigators *speculate* the fire was deliberately started. They emphasized that so far they have no conclusive proof of this theory. . . .

If you can corner an eyewitness or a survivor, see if you can get them to agree to a recorded interview. At this stage, the audience is very interested in the human element in the disaster.

Now that you've made your first preliminary report, don't think your job is over—it is just starting. Now comes the difficult task of digging, searching for more detail, more background, more explanation. Are there any hotel employees around? Can they give you any details as to how many registered guests were in the hotel? Any unusual angles, coincidences, etc.? How do *they* think the fire started? How were the guests warned of the fire? What was the evacuating procedure? Any problems in clearing the hotel? Any damage estimate? Will insurance cover damage? What steps are being taken to care for displaced guests?

Talk to police and find out how the investigation is progressing. Are there any new details? Are there any problems with crowds? How does this fire compare with other fires in the city's history? Is it the worst?

As you gather new information keep reporting back to your newsroom. As word of the disaster spreads through your area, more and more listeners will want to know the latest details. As you prepare each of your new reports (up-dates), emphasize the new developments:

Fire officials now say they have definite proof the fire in the Downtown Hotel was deliberately set. Investigators have uncovered a number of empty gasoline cans in the basement of the 10-story hotel which was gutted by a fire which started less than two hours ago. . . .

After the fire is finally under control, you may be sent home to recuperate or you may be sent to the hospital to check on casualties, or to the makeshift morgue to report on arrangements for handling the dead. You might be dispatched to the fire department to prepare an in-depth report on the arson investigation. It should be perfectly clear that the coverage of a disaster does not end at the scene of the event; each of the ever-widening developments must be investigated and reported.

So far I have been talking about what you should do, but there are things you should avoid doing.

Don't overstate the situation. Don't exaggerate the severity of the disaster which is bad enough without sophomoric dramatics.

Any disaster is rife with rumors, half-truths and unfounded reports; avoid adding the authoritative weight of a news report.

Be sparing in your use of the words *disaster* and *calamity*. Try to avoid adjectives such as *bloody, gory,* etc.

Don't structure your report in such a manner that places blame for the disaster. For example, don't say, ''Five persons were trapped because the hotel had inadequate exits.'' These observations should come later when facts come to light that support such charges.

The disaster may be under control and the police, firemen, and crowds have gone home, but your job is far from over. In the days, weeks, months and even years following a disaster there will be developments that must be covered.

Even if there are no real new developments, there is still a high degree of interest in the disaster, so you will want to keep the story going for a while. It isn't too difficult to develop stories featuring new angles. The major point to remember is to report the latest developments. You don't want to keep beating the same facts, at least not in the same way.

Using the hotel fire as an example, here are some natural follow-up angles you might cover. One of the most frequent types of follow-up stories the morning after a bad fire is the kind that features the following lead:

Firemen are still pouring water on the charred ruins of the Downtown Hotel where four persons lost their lives in a four-alarm fire during the night. . . .

Or, you might emphasize a possible arson investigation:

Fire investigators are poking through the ruins of the Downtown Hotel this morning looking for the possible cause of the four-alarm fire which killed three persons early this morning. . . .

Later in the day, you might "top" the same story with an angle that highlights the condition of the survivors:

> Twenty-three persons are still in critical condition this morning suffering from burns they received during last night's four alarm blaze which gutted the Downtown Hotel. . . .

The story for the noon news might take yet another angle:

> The owners of the Downtown Hotel say their losses will run well over one million dollars. The four-story structure was completely gutted by an early morning blaze which killed four persons and critically injured 23 others. . . .

As you begin preparing for the evening newscast, a check with your sources shows that there have been no new developments in the fire story. To paraphrase an old cliche, *"No* news may be news."

> Fire investigators report no new developments in their search for the arsonist who allegedly touched off that blaze that destroyed the Downtown Hotel early this morning. . . .

In the days following the fire, your new angles might include the continuing investigation, insurance reports, condition of the victims, plans to rebuild the hotel, etc. But it should be pointed out that you can't keep a story "alive" forever. Just because it was a good story last night and is still a good story today doesn't mean it will continue being the most important item in the days to come unless there are important new developments.

The handling of old news raises the interesting question of "What is news?" It is impossible to tell you when a story has lost its news value. This is something that must be felt intuitively; there are no hard and fast guidelines. Generally it can be said that as long as new developments keep cropping up, an event will continue to be of interest to your audience. But when you feel yourself straining for the new angle, it is probably time to drop the item until something else happens.

THE CIVIL DISTURBANCE STORY

In the early days of broadcasting the only civil disturbance that received coverage was war. Now, however, the reports of street battles, riots, civil disturbances, confrontations and other willful large-scale movements and protests are common. Even the smallest city cannot escape militant activity. It is incumbent upon broadcast journalists to know how to handle themselves and their reports when faced with the problem of reporting a civil disturbance. Creating panic and spreading rumors must be avoided at all costs.

Many of the principles that apply to covering disasters also apply to reporting civil disturbances with a few additional points. It should be obvious that the major differences between the two events is simply the distinct possibility of the reporter becoming the physical target for demonstrators. If you are assigned to cover a civil disturbance you must constantly be aware that your life may be in danger, not only from the demonstrators but often, unfortunately, from the police.

This threat of attack from both sides raises the vital question of identifying yourself as a reporter. Should you wear an armband or badge which may make you a target of the mob, or should you go in "undercover" which may result in your being attacked by police who mistake you for a rioter? There is no easy answer. It depends on the situation, but it is a real danger you should be aware of before you decide to wade into the thick of things between the protestors and the police.

The first thing you should do, besides donning your gas mask and riot helmet, is *observe* what is going on: How many protestors? Any violence on *either* side? Any injured police or protestors? Are arrests being made? What type of protest is happening? Is it a violent confrontation or peaceful?

Try and find out who is in command of the official forces. Rely on the command officer or his staff for all announcements. More trouble has been caused by zealous newsmen passing along information and reports that were mere rumors. Substantiate all reports of looting, destruction, mobs, etc.

After the Los Angeles Watts riots, Dr. Theodore Kruglak and Dr. Kenneth Harwood of the University of Southern California conferred with reporters who had covered the violence, and then drew up the following guidelines which would go a long way towards making the media a more responsible partner in handling riot situations:

1. Avoid emphasizing stories on public tensions while the tensions of a particular incident are developing. Ask the law enforcement agency involved whether the developing incident is designated as a disturbance of the peace or otherwise. Report the official designation of the incident.
2. Your reports should not state the exact location, intersection, street name or number until authorities have sufficient personnel on hand to maintain control.
3. Immediate or direct reporting from the scene should minimize interpretation, eliminate airing of rumors, and avoid using unverified statements.
4. Avoid trivial incidents.
5. Because inexpert use of cameras, bright lights, or microphones may stir exhibitionism, great care should be exercised. Because too, of the danger of injury or even death to news personnel, their presence should be as unobtrusive as possible. Unmarked vehicles should be used for initial evaluation of events of this nature.

6. Cruising in an area of potential crisis may invite trouble. Reporters should make full use of the law enforcement headquarters nearest such an area until a newsworthy event occurs.
7. Reporters at the scene of an explosive or potentially explosive situation should avoid reporting of interviews with obvious inciters.
8. Reporters should inform in advance any person who is interviewed that the interview may be made public.
9. Scare headlines, scare bulletins and sensationalism of other kinds should be avoided by all media.
10. All news media should make every effort to assure that only seasoned reporters are sent to the scene of a disaster.
11. No reporter should use superlatives or adjectives which might incite or enlarge a conflict, or cause renewal of trouble in areas where disturbances have been quieted.
12. Advisory data for discretionary use by reporters should be written in calm, matter-of-fact sentences. This is to avoid inflammatory results from unintended public reporting of discretionary material.
13. Reporters should not detail how any weapon is made, obtained or used.
14. Reporters should not identify precise locations of command posts of public officials, police, fire units or military units.
15. Reporters must govern their actions by the rules of good taste, common decency, and common sense.

The above guidelines are valuable for reporting civil disturbances, but they do not include what may be the most important rule: reporting the full context of the situation. That is, you must make it clear that only a small minority was rioting, or that the majority of a community is working to halt the militant activity. Above all, the media must try to analyze the reasons for the unrest and what can be done to bring the violence to an end.[1]

THE TERRORIST STORY

You're working the afternoon shift, getting ready for the evening newscast when the telephone rings. You pick up the receiver and a gruff voice speaks.

"I'm holding three people hostage. I've got the place wired with dynamite. One false move and they're all dead. I want to talk to the President of the United States. If I don't hear from him in two hours I will blow their heads off. . . ."

Usually terrorist activity, whatever its political or social motivation, in-

---

Similar guidelines have been adopted by the Northern California Chapter of the Radio-TV News Directors Association as well as other chapters of the RTNDA.

volves the taking of hostages or the seizing of property and the demand for media coverage. The threat of violence is used to "buy" media access and you, as a reporter, may face the serious problem of acting as a media "go-between" linking the terrorist with the public.

What should you do in such a situation? How do you balance your professional responsibilities as a broadcast journalist and the lives of hostages which may be dependent on your skillful handling of those making the threats?

There are no simple answers. Each situation will be different and will demand specific responses and attitudes. Your maturity and sense of professionalism will meet their strongest challenge in a terrorist situation. I can only suggest you carefully consider the guidelines issued by CBS news as a relatively safe procedure for making your final decision as to what to do:

"(1). An essential component of the story is the demands of the terrorist/kidnapper, and we must report these demands. But we should avoid providing an excessive platform for the terrorist/kidnapper. Thus, unless such demands are succinctly stated and free of rhetoric and propaganda, it may be better to paraphrase the demands instead of presenting them directly through the voice or picture of the terrorist/kidnapper.

"(2). Except in the most compelling circumstances, and then only with the approval of the president of CBS News or in his absence the senior vice president of news, there should be no live coverage of the terrorist/kidnapper since we may fall into the trap of providing an unedited platform for him. (This does not limit live, on-the-spot reporting by CBS News reporters, but care should be exercised to assure restraint and context.)

"(3). News personnel should be mindful of the probable need by the authorities who are dealing with the terrorist for communication by telephone and hence should endeavor to ascertain, wherever feasible, whether our own use of such lines would be likely to interfere with the authorities' communications.

"(4). Responsible CBS News representatives should endeavor to contact experts dealing with the hostage situation to determine whether they have any guidance on such questions as phraseology to be avoided, what kind of questions or reports might tend to exacerbate the situation, etc. Any such recommendations by established authorities on the scene should be carefully considered as guidance (but not as instruction) by CBS News personnel.

"(5). Local authorities should also be given the name or names of CBS personnel whom they can contact should they have further guidance or wish to deal with such delicate questions as a newsman's call to the terrorists or other matters which might interfere with authorities dealing with the terrorists.

"(6). Guidelines affecting our coverage of civil disturbances are also applicable here, especially those which relate to avoid use of inflammatory catch words or phrases, the reporting of rumors, etc. As in the case of policy dealing with civil disturbances, in dealing with a hostage story, reporters should obey all

---

* From *Broadcasting* Magazine, April 18, 1977.

olice instructions but report immediately to their superiors any such instructions
hich may seem to be intended to manage or suppress the news.

"(7). Coverage of this kind of story should be in such over-all balance as
 length, that it does not unduly crowd out other important news of the
our/day."

It is impossible to predict the results of terrorist coverage. But it is a ques-
on you must face if you are involved in covering such an incident.

6

A Journalist's Rights and Responsibilities

The First Amendment of the Constitution says plainly that there shall be no law abridging the freedom of the press. Even though the protection seems simple and complete, court interpretations over the years have created complex and often confusing laws governing the work of a journalist.

Since laws pertaining to communications are constantly being affected by court rulings, it is impossible to be precise when discussing the legal constraints you must deal with as a journalist. However, it is imperative that you be aware of these various laws and judicial interpretations so you may not stumble blindly into legal action which could prove costly and possibly damaging to your career.

The information in this chapter is not meant to be a complete guide to communications law; the outcome of any specific incident will inevitably depend on court rulings which can be very unpredictable.

LIBEL AND SLANDER

The most common problem area for journalists are the laws defining libel and slander. There are no federal libel laws. Each state has its own statutes, and what is libel in one state may be perfectly legal in another. We can only rely on the most recent U.S. Supreme Court decisions to give some indication of what is generally considered libelous material with a warning that you should make sure of the restrictions applicable in your state.

It is important to know about libel for two reasons: (1) so you will know what you can't say, and (2) so you will know what you can say. The later reason is probably the most important since many beginning reporters are "gun shy when it comes to handling a delicate story because they have been terrified of the possible consequences of libel without really understanding what they can report with impunity.

While libel laws may vary, the following definition which is given in the *American and English Encyclopedia of Law* covers most of the general points of libel:

> A libel is a malicious defamation expressed either by writing, printing, or pictures which tends to blacken the memory of one who is dead, or to impeach the honesty, integrity, virtue, or reputation, or to publish the natural or alleged defects of one who is alive and thereby expose him to public hatred, contempt, or ridicule; or to cause him to be shunned or avoided, or to injure him in his office, business, or occupation.

Slander is the spoken form of libel. This distinction raises an interesting question. Is defamation by radio-TV slander or libel? There has not been a simple court ruling on this matter, but most courts seem to be leaning towards defining radio-TV defamation as libel since the damaging material was originally prepared in written form. It should also be pointed out that the penalties for libel are usually heavier than for slander because the courts assume the potential for damage is greater by the printed word than by the spoken word. Broadcasting has become recognized as an effective medium, potentially as dangerous as the print media and therefore the dissemination of libelous material must be dealt with severely.

Looking at the definition again, it is apparent that there are four distinct parts that comprise a libelous statement:

1. *Any statement which falsely accuses a person of suffering from some loathsome or contagious disease.* It has been held that it is libel to accuse a person of suffering from a disease such as smallpox, leprosy, venereal disease, and the like. The theory is that such an accusation would cause the person to be shunned and avoided by society.

2. *Any statement which falsely accuses a person of unfitness to conduct his business or profession.* The statement must affect the person named in a trade or profession in which he is actually engaged. To say a physician is unfit to practice law would not be libelous.

3. *Any statement which falsely accuses a person of a crime.* A false statement that the plaintiff is guilty of murder, rape, arson, larceny, etc. would be libelous and would be grounds for a court case even without proof of damage on the part of the one accused.

4. *Any false statement which upon its face brings disgrace or ridicule upon the party accused.* This point is the "elastic clause" which covers those specific situations not outlined above. An example would be accusing someone of indiscriminate sexual relations even if such activity is not illegal.

Not only is a definition of libel difficult but so, too, is anticipating the result of legal action. Court interpretations of libel laws are undergoing constant revision. The 1974 ruling by the U.S. Supreme Court in *Gertz* v. *Robert Welch, Inc.* provides the most recent thinking on the matter.

The case involved a Chicago attorney, Elmer Gertz, who had been retained in a civil suit filed by a Chicago policeman convicted of murder. The attorney was featured in an article in *American Opinion,* a John Birch Society magazine that accused Gertz of being a "Leninist," "a Communist-fronter," and otherwise questioned his loyalty.

In defense against the suit filed by Gertz, the magazine's managing editor stated he had no reason not to believe the story filed by a free-lancer, and further claimed the attorney was a public figure and the magazine was merely commenting on a matter of public concern. By showing this, he hoped to establish "privilege" requiring Gertz to prove "reckless disregard" which the plaintiff could not do.

The trial judge ruled against Gertz saying that since the lawyer was a private citizen he had to prove "actual malice" to receive punitive damages. When the case reached the Supreme Court, the judges disagreed, saying that private citizens speaking on public issues do not have to prove actual malice. In short, a mixed blessing for the journalist attempting to avoid libel actions. While making it easier for private citizens to collect damages, the Court made it more difficult for public figures. Although the question of who is a public figure is still clouded (see Invasion of Privacy on p. 98), the Court ruled that punitive damages cannot be awarded unless the plaintiff proves actual malice. The reasoning of the Court follows rulings by several states which have forbidden punitive damages, saying they can be used selectively to punish unpopular ideas.

The Gertz case also undercut the long-standing common law definition of libel *per se.* It is no longer possible for the plaintiff to simply argue that certain words are defamatory, and as a result, damages should be awarded.

The decision also indicates the Court will narrowly define "public figure." Since such people must still establish malice to win punitive damages, the distinction between public and private is essential to journalists.

According to Justice Powell's majority opinion, the public figure differs from the private person because public figures "thrust themselves to the forefront of particular public controversies in order to influence the resolution of the issues involved."

However, many persons mentioned in your newscasts fall into gray areas between "public" and "private." Since the Court granted each state the right to more clearly define "public figures," each case must be decided on its own merits.

Despite the confusion that exists over libel laws, the Gertz case makes a few things clear: private citizens will find it easier to sustain libel actions but punitive damages will be difficult to recover; and libel *per se* laws are awaiting interpretation by state courts.

Recent authorities have suggested a three-fold classification of potentially libelous statements. In his book, *The Rights and Privileges of the Press,* Fred Siebert gives three levels of public statements:

1. Obviously innocent.
2. Questionable. A jury must decide.
3. Obviously defamatory. No injury must be shown.

Even with this breakdown, there is still no reliable yardstick against which to judge the potential libel in a statement. Anyone may sue you for libel. Whether they collect damages will be decided by a court of law.

Most reporters approach the danger limits of libel when dealing with crime news; and there are certain things that, if avoided, will lessen the risk of libel suits:

1. Don't refer to a man as a suspected slayer when he is just picked up for questioning about a murder.
2. Don't call a man a killer when he is arrested on a homicide charge.
3. Even if the suspect confesses, do not call him a criminal. The confession may be inadmissible evidence and he may be acquitted.
4. Be careful about using police statements accusing someone of guilt. The use of the word "alleged" is no guarantee of immunity from a libel suit.
5. Avoid statements which attack a person's moral character.

There are five possible defenses against libel:

1. *Truth:* The best defense is that a statement about the plaintiff is true. It is a complete defense unless malice can be proven.

You must not only know the truth of your statements, but must be able to prove them to the satisfaction of the court. It is not a defense to claim the libel was broadcast upon the authority of a third person (a public speaker, the wire services, even the network). The plaintiff can sue both the individual making the statement and all stations which carry it.

2. *Privilege:* A statement is considered privileged if it is extracted from public records, documents, hearings, or testimony. But the release of information before a public hearing has been held is not privileged nor is the information contained in police reports.

3. *Fair comment:* Everyone has the right to criticize or comment on matters of public interest and concern, provided such statements meet four basic tests:

a) The statement must be on a matter of public interest such as comments on public affairs, public officials, artistic performances, etc.
b) The statement must be fair. This question is usually decided by a jury. Therefore, you must be careful before you attempt to ascertain motives for a public action.
c) The statement must be without malice. You have no right to be using the occasion to promote anything other than fair comment.
d) The statement must, in fact, be comment and not allegation of fact. In other words, the privilege of fair comment does not give you the right to make libelous statements about an allegation of fact.

4. *Absence of malice:* As pointed out in the review of the Gertz decision, malice is an important ingredient in any libel suit, especially one involving a

public figure. The plaintiff in a suit must prove the presence of malice—a for-midable task. The defendant may show the following points in attempting to es-tablish absence of malice:

   a) There is general cause to believe the charges are true.
   b) That rumors to the same effect as the libelous statement had long been common knowledge.
   c) That the libelous statement came from another source previously be-lieved to be correct.
   d) That the plaintiff's character was generally bad.
   e) That an immediate retraction, correction or apology was made.
   f) That the statement was broadcast in the heat of a political campaign.
   g) That the statement had been made to the plaintiff and he did not deny it before broadcast.

5. *Retraction:* Often you can avoid a suit by prompt retraction of the state-ment. If a suit does result, such a retraction may mitigate the damages. In some states a complete retraction is a complete defense against libel suits.

INVASION OF PRIVACY

One of the rights guaranteed Americans is the freedom to be left alone, safe from public display and criticism of private matters. Numerous Supreme Court decisions have attempted to define the balance between the public's right to know and an individual's right to secrecy. This distinction is important because serious litigation can result from your innocent story which violates the subject's right of privacy.

How, then, do you tell what is legitimate public concern and what is not? In 1976, the U.S. Supreme Court, wrestling with the same question, upheld a Florida Supreme Court decision limiting the scope of legitimate media reporting. In the case, *Time* magazine, in reporting the divorce of Russell and Mary Fire-stone, erroneously stated adultery as the grounds for the divorce. During the trial, the Time-Life lawyers argued the divorce was a public event of great con-cern and therefore malice would have to be proved. The state court held, and the Supreme Court agreed, that the divorce action was not of significant newsworth-iness and Time-Life could not seek First Admendment protection.

Everything you write is potential fodder for an invasion of privacy suit. Definitions continue to be issued by the Supreme Court but they only raise new questions. To be safe, you should think carefully about using items that deal with persons not in the public eye. These private citizens, unable to use the media to refute negative information, are afforded greater protection under the law; they do not have to prove malice to collect general damages. If your stories deal with people accustomed to wide media exposure, your chances of running afoul of privacy laws are reduced.

For example, you would be safe in writing an item regarding your mayor's off-duty drinking bouts if they influenced his public performance of his job. However, you might run into serious trouble if you reported on his brother's penchant for gambling. Privacy is a hazy concept. When in doubt about the propriety of a news item, whether it's one you've prepared or one sent by the press associations, your best tactic is to wait. Your concern should indicate the potential for a law suit. Any story that causes you to hesitate is never important enough that it can't be postponed until you have time to check with your superiors. After all, your employers will be your co-defendants. You owe them the privilege of using your best professional judgment.

SHIELD LAWS

In the last two decades, there has been a growing conflict between reporters and government agencies over a journalist's right to protect news sources. Local, state and federal investigative groups have demanded that reporters give detailed testimony about their sources. Some newspersons have been put in jail, charged with contempt of court, for refusing to disclose such information. And such cases prompted action by professional journalism groups—Sigma Delta Chi (SDX) and the Radio-Television News Directors Association (RTNDA), as well as the American Civil Liberties Union (ACLU) and others—to demand the passage of "shield laws" to protect newsmen from legal action.

So far, about 12 states have given protection to journalists. However, even in these states immunity is not complete. Many of the laws contain conditions which permit judges wide latitude in interpreting the circumstances of individual cases. This elasticity, some journalists claim, makes such "shield" laws worthless, while others insist complete protection would open the way for irresponsible reporting.

Since "shield" laws vary from state to state, it is impossible to offer specific guidelines on handling source confidentiality. The outcome of any particular incident will depend on the case, the local political situation, the disposition of the judge, the strength of the Grand Jury, and your willingness to resist or cooperate.

As a reporter, you must decide if you are willing to go to jail to protect a news source. This is a question only you can answer; but answer it you must before promising secrecy in exchange for information.

In 1970, the U.S. Court of Appeals ruled that the federal government must show a pressing need for evidence before ordering a journalist to testify before a Grand Jury. The court ruled that the reporter's information and sources are privileged unless the information is otherwise unobtainable and is necessary for the government's purpose. The ruling gave the final responsibility for determining specific cases to the courts.

The Court's action means that the federal government retains the power to limit a reporter's right to protect news sources if it is determined the needs of the state are more important. Thus, a reporter has no guarantee of immunity—only an implied promise.

SUNSHINE LAWS

Paralleling the increased concern about a reporter's right to protect sources has been action to ensure journalistic access to governmental proceedings. Almost every state and the federal government have enacted legislation to guarantee "freedom of information" for private citizens and reporters. Although the specific laws vary widely in their impact, governmental information is generally becoming easier to obtain. The passage of so-called "sunshine laws" forbidding the holding of secret governmental meetings and decisions, except in limited circumstances provides additional authority for you to report on almost all aspects of governmental operations.

However, your right to exercise this privilege will depend on local laws and your willingness to pursue reluctant government officials in demanding allegiance to the intent of the legislation.

If you are being kept in the dark about the activities of a governmental agency despite "freedom of information" statutes, you can emphasize this fact in your reports on the matter which will alert citizens to the issue and, perhaps, generate sufficient public pressure to force public disclosure.

SECTION 315A AND THE FAIRNESS DOCTRINE

Broadcast journalists, unlike newspaper and magazine reporters, have additional restrictions on their freedom since broadcasting is under the direct control and supervision of the Federal Communications Commission.

While there are an infinite variety of commission regulations governing the technical and commercial aspects of broadcasting, Section 315a and The Fairness Doctrine, which outline your responsibilities in covering political candidates and controversial issues, are of particular importance.

Recognizing the particular power of radio and television to influence public opinion, federal legislation was passed limiting the involvement of broadcasters in political campaigns. One part of the Communications Act insists political advertising be made equally available to all candidates running for the same office. This is not ordinarily the concern of the journalist since political appearances on newscasts are not considered advertising but legitimate coverage of the day's events. In fact, court decisions have totally removed regularly scheduled news programs and interview shows such as "Meet the Press" from the guidelines established by Section 315a.

However, this does not mean you are free to report political races without regard to fair and impartial coverage of all candidates. Allocating a disproportionate amount of time to one candidate over opponents can result in your running afoul of the Fairness Doctrine which is the FCC's attempt to encourage fair unbiased reporting of important social or political issues.

It is difficult to define "fair, unbiased reporting." Depending on the public's attitude on a particular issue, your reports can be praised as "totally accurate" or attacked as "totally dishonest." Any time you report on a socially significant event, you run the risk of being accused of violating the Fairness Doctrine. The only protection available is a constant professional awareness and close monitoring of your reportage to provide the most balanced story possible.

Neither Section 315a nor the Fairness Doctrine restrict your right to prepare and broadcast *editorial comment* on public issues if such programming is clearly labeled as such and equal time is offered for rebuttal by opponents of your viewpoint. FCC regulations spell out the specific procedure to be followed for broadcasting editorials. If they are followed, there is little chance of becoming involved in legal action.

Although it is difficult to define "objective reporting," the FCC is quite adamant about how journalists handle controversial topics—especially those reports that include attacks against specific persons or groups. If your newscast includes such material, it is your legal responsibility to contact the person attacked, provide a transcript of the charge and allow equal time for a response.

It should be mentioned that you will have more difficulty with station management over coverage of controversial issues than with the public. Unless, you are fully aware of Section 315a and the Fairness Doctrine, you will be unable to support your attempts to cover such topics since management is reluctant to become embroiled in controversy that could lead to legal action.

However, if you keep abreast of the latest FCC rulings in these areas, you should have little legal difficulty covering controversial stories. Accept the rules as a challenge to present balanced coverage and you will satisfy the FCC requirements and the public's need to keep abreast on important topics.

By this time, you are probably afraid to write anything—I hope not. I have not presented information about the possible legal pitfalls in reporting to frighten you, but merely to make you aware of the penalities for improper reporting.

To be safe without getting bogged down in complex legal terminology, remember these points:

1. Use common sense, fair play and stick to objective facts.
2. Don't call anybody anything unsavory.
3. Make sure questionable material is privileged, within the bounds of fair comment, or true and without malice.
4. When in doubt about a story, don't use it. You may miss a good item but you may save yourself from a libel suit.

7

Good Taste in Broadcast News

IN THE MINDS OF MANY LISTENERS and reporters there seems to be a natural link between good taste and libel. You can think of good taste as a sort of libel without the legal restrictions.

Defining good taste is difficult, if not impossible. Your definition must be based on a variety of factors such as audience characteristics, area of the country, environment of audience, etc. What is considered good taste this year was considered in poor taste 50 years ago. What is objectionable to an 80-year-old might be perfectly acceptable to a teenager. What might go unnoticed by an urban audience might cause great concern to a rural listener. In short, the bounds of good taste are flexible and ever changing.

It can be argued that good taste doesn't change over the years, but rather it is our conception of what constitutes good taste that undergoes periodic revision. It is probable that what we consider taboo today will be commonplace a decade from now. Twenty years ago, it was considered almost obscene to use the word *rape* on the air. We relied on terms like *criminally assaulted, molested,* and *violated* to convey the idea. Now the use of such substitutes would raise curious eyebrows as the audience wondered what we were trying to say.

Even if we accept the fact that the concept of good taste is ever changing, there are still certain guideposts that broadcast journalists should obey if only because radio-TV is much more of a mass media than the motion picture, magazine, or stage play where you can restrict the audience to ''adults only.'' Radio and TV, unlike the other media, go into the home with no restrictions. They are family media, which demand discretion. You never know who will be listening.

Obscenity and profanity are barred from the air by federal law under the threat of a massive fine and prison sentence. Other terms and phrases offensive to the general public must be controlled by the dictates of good taste.

Not all news is "good" or "nice." Much of it deals with unpleasant subject matter: murder, rape, riots, fires, etc. These are the staple fare of the newspapers which revel in the gore of man's inhumanity to man. But radio has more impact than the written word. It can incite riots and raise passions. So the ethical broadcast journalist must avoid inflammatory verbs, sensational adjectives and lurid details.

It used to be that such words as *hell* and *damn* were totally banned from radio. But common practice is to allow such terms especially when they are an integral part of a direct quote from a news source. President Harry Truman was noted for his colorful use of the English language. His speech was often liberally sprinkled with a good share of *hell's* and *damn's*. It would have been ridiculous to rewrite his promise to give someone hell to giving him heck. I am not suggesting that you include such terms in a story as a matter of course. They should only be used when it is an essential part of a direct quote.

It is possible that as the years pass stronger words will become accepted in broadcast journalism. But for now, you're inviting trouble and criticism if you use such terms. It is far better to try and write around a profane word or phrase than to risk the ire of some offended listeners or the FCC.

As the press associations have pointed out, it is impossible to set down any regulations on the matter of good taste. But there are certain areas that must be handled with care.

Physical and Mental Handicaps: Avoid mentioning handicaps unless they are an integral part of the story. Never poke fun at a handicapped person.

Sex: Sex crimes, unfortunately, are part of our daily lives. We can't ignore them, but broadcast journalists must avoid wallowing in the sordid details of the event. It is sufficient to mention that a victim was raped, you don't have to explain how.

Race and Color: Sometimes race is an integral part of a story especially when a member of that race has done something that is unusual for that group such as being the first Black to be elected mayor of a large American city. But unless the person's race helps explain the significance of the event, it is good taste to leave it out.

A Missouri news director, Rod Gelatt of KOMU-TV, explained to a group of student journalists once that the constant mention of race in news stories may simply be a matter of habit:

> I hadn't been in Virginia very long before I found myself striking out the word *Negro* in countless news stories. The reporters couldn't see why, and it took me a long time to appreciate their views on this. To those southern boys, it was just as acceptable to use *Negro* in any story dealing with a Negro—whether the story was of a racial nature or not—as it was my experience not to use a racial description.

Age: Unless it is essential to the story, a person's age is a private matter.

Religion: Like race, religion should only be mentioned when it is a necessary detail which will explain the story. Sometimes a religious leader runs afoul of the law and it is impossible to avoid mentioning religious affiliation, but it is important to avoid casting an unfavorable light.

Crime: Law breaking is probably the major news item in this country. There is no way to avoid it. But you should play down the sensational details. Write it as straight as possible without your words dripping blood. If a man hacks his wife to death with a butcher knife (which happens more often than you would believe), the public is entitled to know. But omit a word picture of the blood-dripping knife, the crimson-soaked sheets, the dismembered corpse.

If a man commits suicide, write about it. But leave the broken neck, protruding tongue and blue face to the newspapers.

Even with these general guidelines, good taste will still remain a matter of personal judgment. As in the case of libel, the best protection against offending public decency is common sense, realizing what is generally acceptable.

In addition to the problem of good taste, there are some other general rules to observe in broadcast journalism. For example, when reporting a suicide avoid glorifying it as a justifiable solution. It is possible that your story will prompt another troubled soul to seek the same answer. You should also play down the suicide angle as much as possible. The important fact is that the person is dead—the cause is secondary:

> **POOR:** A 45-year old local man . . . Thomas Newman . . . committed suicide today by jumping off the Golden Gate Bridge.
>
> **BETTER:** A 45-year old local man . . . Thomas Newman . . . fell to his death from the Golden Gate Bridge today. The County Coroner ruled his death a suicide.

The second version is more acceptable for two reasons: (1) It downplays the suicide aspect, and (2) the cause of death is attributed to the coroner. The second point is the most important. Make sure the death is a suicide before you say so. The coroner, or the medical examiner, is the only one who can officially declare a death a suicide. This is important because there are many accidental deaths that resemble suicides, and if you say they are and the coroner disagrees with your speculation you might find yourself embroiled in a law suit.

Another problem area is medical news. It is essential that you develop a healthy skepticism about all newly reported medical cures and treatments. Today's miracle cure may be tomorrow's discarded theory.

Related to the problem of reporting medical news is the general rule about using the names of professionals such as doctors, clergymen and attorneys. In a word, *don't.* Ordinarily, unless the professional has made the news for something of their own doing, it is considered unethical to use their name if they're merely acting in a professional capacity. For example, if you check with a doctor about the condition of a patient and use a statement in your story, simply say "the patient's doctor says"; nothing more is needed.

Broadcast journalists must be aware that there are some words and expressions which are dangerous to use, not in the sense of libel, but because of the re-action they may produce.

I am talking about those words whose connotations are a bit too colorful and whose use must be carefully reviewed. For instance, when you speak of a disturbance avoid calling it a riot. This term conjures up a mental image in the minds of your listeners which may be far worse than the actual situation. You say "explosion" when you mean a "fire" and the audience is led to believe the worst. There are a number of these words which, when used improperly, can leave a wrong and sometimes dangerous impression.

Be cautious about the practice of breaking into regular programming with a news bulletin or flash. If you do it too often, you will become like the boy who yelled "wolf" once too often; your important news "flashes" will soon lose their impact.

As you will find out, the wire services are a bit lax in their use of "bulle-tin" and "flash" news items; you shouldn't be. Even though the wire services may slug a story as a "bulletin," most of the time it probably deserves nothing more than a "we have this late word" inserted during a regularly scheduled newscast.

There are some 600,000 words in the English language, about 50,000 of which are used occasionally, and 6,000 of which are used frequently. Some-where in that vocabulary there are enough acceptable words to substitute for those terms which offend public decency.

8

Putting Together the Five Minute Newscast

SO FAR I HAVE BEEN LOOKING at the various parts of a news story prepared for broadcast. In this chapter I shall show how to put all these various items together to form a complete newscast. For simplicity's sake I will only construct a five minute 'cast although the principles involved apply equally to all newscasts regardless of length.

1. The first thing to do is to read all the copy available, local and wire, and categorize it according to your own breakdown. A convenient arrangement might include: state, local, national, international, sports, weather, business, Washington, politics, etc. Don't worry about formal categories and overlapping; the important thing is to familiarize yourself with what is available.

As you go through this sorting process, you can save yourself time by discarding duplicate reports, out-dated items and other stories you know won't be used.

Since the wire services are constantly updating their reports, it is essential that you read from the earliest to the latest report on each story so that you can be aware of the trend in the event and to find out details that the first reports might carry but which may be dropped later in the day.

2. You know how many lines of radio copy takes a minute of air time and you know how much time you have to fill, so it's a simple matter of multiplying the air time by your lines per minute to find out how much copy you will need. Once this has been determined you can choose which stories you will use and assign a certain time to each so the newscast will exactly fill the allotted time. Don't forget to include your open and close, commercials, coupling pins and other program material that might be included within the time allotted for the newscast.

3. By now you should have a very specific idea of what you want to feature in the 'cast and how you are going to play each item. At this stage all that is left is the task of writing and editing the news to the number of lines assigned to each item. Arrange the stories in the decided order, write the necessary coupling pins, tape introductions and the like, and you are ready to go on the air.

This procedure will be a bit clearer by looking at a specific five minute newscast for a local radio station. The editor, getting ready to prepare the newscast, knew she had more than three hours of wire copy and another 30 minutes of local news to pare down to fit the 'cast. Her reading speed was 15 lines a minute and she knew the open and close plus the commercial took a minute and a half. This left her three and a half minutes for the news, which means she could write 52.5 lines of copy.

With that limit in mind, the editor read all the available copy. She separated it into the appropriate categories, culling out the less important and repetitive copy. This left her with the following items she considered important:

Congress Adjourns . . . . National
City council election . . . . Local
Governor arrives . . . . Local
School holiday starts . . . . Local
Local sports . . . . Local
Weather . . . . Local

From past experience, the editor knew the weather could be handled in five lines (20 seconds) which left her 3:10 for the other items. She also knew the sports story wouldn't change and needed another five lines giving her 2:50.

Then came the writing of the stories and the insertion of the coupling pins which worked out to 45 lines or 10 seconds over her alloted time. She decided not to cut any copy, figuring she could pick up the time by reading a bit faster through the entire newscast.

You will notice that the first thing the editor did was to time the last two items in the 'cast. This "backtiming" simply means the editor actually reads the last items against a stopwatch, marking the required time on each of the backtimed items. She then knew that she must have exactly a certain amount of time to finish the newscast "on the nose." Backtiming avoids the necessity of stretching or rushing at the end of the newscast since you know that if the last item takes 20 seconds and the close 30 seconds, you must start reading it at 4:10 into the newscast to come out on time. This allows you to cut short a story if you are running long, or read some "pad" copy if you see you will come out short. At the appropriate moment you simply pick up the backtimed item, which you had previously set to the side, start reading, and end the 'cast right on time.

9

The Mini-Documentary

The mini-documentary is a new development in broadcast news. Faced with the realization that 30- and 60-minute news features were no longer keeping the interest of listeners, broadcast news executives introduced the concept of "serialized" news reports.

Instead of devoting a half-hour, for example, to a single subject, the material is presented in a series of mini-documentaries (usually 3½ minutes) aired throughout the broadcast schedule. Thus a modern listener, unwilling to devote a solid block of time to a report on a subject, is given the information in smaller, easier-to-digest, and less boring chapters.

The radio mini-documentary, pioneered by stations featuring all-news formats and now being used by many major market stations and the networks, is an excellent opportunity for you to devote more time to a particular subject of local importance or interest without drastically interrupting your regular format.

The best way to understand the production problems involved with mini-documentaries is to give you detailed analysis of a specific assignment. While many productions will involve a similar procedure, remember that each story is unique and will demand a structure most suited to the particular issue and how you choose to present it. My example is only that—an example.

A successful mini-documentary involves careful planning throughout the entire process from the inception of the story idea to the final script. While it's possible to get away with "last minute" preparation for a five-minute newscast, shoddy workmanship becomes painfully obvious during a program series.

As an example, I was once assigned the task of doing a five-part series on drug abuse in local high schools. I was told each segment would be three minutes long and aired three times each day. This meant the series would be broadcast three times over a five-day period.

Setting aside the series format until the writing stage, I investigated the subject in the same way I handled a normal news story. I was not concerned about the program format until I finished gathering interviews and facts. Once I completed the research, the material suggested a "natural" organization:

Program One: Overview of the Local Problem—include statistics from police, health, drug abuse office, etc.

Program Two: Drugs in School—interviews with teachers, principals, counsellors.

Program Three: Kids Look at Drugs—interviews with young drug users.

Program Four: Parents and Drugs—interviews with parents of drug users.

Program Five: What Can Be Done?—interviews with drug abuse experts, doctors, ex-junkies, etc.

Although mini-documentaries demand the same professional approach as regular news reports, more attention must be paid to "selling" the entire series to the audience. This is best accomplished by writing an introduction that briefly outlines the intent of the entire program and offers listeners a reason to tune in. A separate introduction should be written for each show so "first time listeners" will not be confused.

Program One: This city has a serious drug problem in its senior and junior high schools. According to police records, one of every three 6th-graders has either smoked marijuana, taken LSD, swallowed tranquilizers or gotten drunk on hard liquor. This program is the first in a series of five to deal with the problem of teen-age drug abuse in our city. Following reports . . . which can be heard three times a day through Friday . . . will look closely at why kids take drugs, what the drugs are doing to them, and what can be done about the problem.

Program Two: Our city's teen-agers have a drug problem. Since they spend most of their time in school, teachers, principals and counsellors have a unique perspective on the drug situation. In today's program . . . the second in a five-part series on teen-age drug abuse . . . we will look at the classroom and drugs. Following reports . . . which can be heard three times a day through Friday . . . will look at other aspects of the problem.

Program Three: Teachers, parents, police. They say our city has a teen-age drug problem. The teenagers? They deny it. In this, the third program in a five-part series on teen-age drug abuse, we will listen to teenagers talking about their experiences with drugs. The remaining programs . . .

which can be heard daily through Friday . . . will feature the parents' view and advice from health authorities.

Program Four: Everyone knows a kid has a drug problem before his parents. Yet, parents are the ones who have the most difficulty dealing with drugs. This fourth program in a five-part series on drug abuse features the comments of mothers and fathers who have faced a child using drugs. Tomorrow's program will present suggestions from health authorities on coping with drug abuse.

Program Five: There is no doubt that our city has a teen-age drug abuse problem. To find out what can be done to deal with the issues we have raised in the last four parts of this five-part series, we discussed alternatives with a wide range of experts.

Each introduction is about 15-seconds long yet provides an overview of each segment, a reminder of the entire series, and a "tease" for subsequent programs. As previously mentioned, mini-documentary production is an exacting process demanding the most efficent use of time possible.

Not only do the introductions serve the needs of an audience, but they also provide a fairly exact writing outline to make it easier to handle each program's news content as a separate item.

After completing the body of each story, I must write a conclusion, to give a quick review of the program, a reminder of the entire series, and a tease for the next presentation. Like introductions, conclusions can be written before preparing each story or they can be allowed to evolve from the story material itself. I prefer to allow each report to suggest its own conclusion. The chances of it sounding forced or artificial are thus greatly reduced. The following are the conclusions prepared for the drug abuse series:

Program One: There can be no doubt . . . at least in the minds of authorities . . . that our city has a teen-age drug abuse problem. As indicated, the schools are the center of most illegal drug use. In tomorrow's program . . . the second in this five-part series . . we will talk to teachers, principals and counsellors about drug use in junior and senior high school.

Program Two: To teachers, drug use is a serious problem crippling the student's ability to learn. Do students agree? Tomorrow's program . . . the third in a five-part series . . . will feature interviews with some of this city's teen-agers about the way they use drugs.

Program Three: While some teen-agers insist drugs are no problem, their parents express worry and sometimes panic about drugs.

What are parents afraid of? How have they dealt with drug use? Tommorrow's program . . . the fourth in a five-part series . . . includes interviews with parents who have faced drug use in their families.

Program Four: What can be done to overcome the fears parents have about drug use by their children? No-one has a guaranteed answer, but tomorrow's program . . . the last in this five-part series . . . will offer some suggestions from a wide range of authorities.

Program Five: During this five-part series, we have seen that drug use by our city's teen-agers is a problem with no easy solutions. Even getting all to agree on the important issues is difficult. However, one suggestion seems worthy of consideration . . . increased public discussion. Today's program and the other four in this series were presented to further this goal. Your comments are welcome. Next week, we will take an in-depth look at another problem facing today's teenager . . . the rise in early marriages.

If your station does not present mini-documentaries, you should encourage such programming whenever possible since most five-minute news formats do a poor job of presenting detailed reports. In addition, the longer form is an opportunity to be more creative than normally demanded by regularly scheduled newscasts. Don't let the length of a series intimidate you. If each segment is handled like a normal news item and your introductions/conclusions are properly prepared, you should have no difficulty exploring the potential of this new development in broadcast news.

Appendices

APPENDIX A
Style Guide

1. Use only one side of standard 8½ × 11-inch copy paper.
2. Triple space all copy.
3. Type either all capitals or "up and down" depending on preference of news department.
4. Set margins for a 70-space line (between 10 and 80). This will give you an average of 10 words per line which works out to about 15 lines per minute depending on the announcer's reading speed. For television, set the left margin at 35 for the audio part of the script. This gives you about 6 words to a line or 21 lines a minute.
5. In the upper right-hand corner of the first page of each story you should have the following information:

> Plane Crash ("slug line"—few words describing story)
> 6/24/70 (date)
> 11:00 news (identify which newscast if you broadcast more than one)
> Jones (your name)

6. On succeeding pages you should put only the page number and the slug line in the upper right corner.

> Plane Crash
> Add one (. . . add two . . . add three . . . etc.)

7. Indicate the end of a story by some mark that your department designates. Universally accepted are the #### and —30—.

8. If the story takes more than one page you should write MORE (in capitals) on the bottom of each page and observe the following special rules:

    a. Do not split sentences from one page to the next.
    b. Do not split words from one page to the next.

9. Write only one story per page, unless you are preparing a round-up of related items. When writing a round-up, however, each story must be separate paragraphs set apart by end marks (### or—30—) after each story.
10. Leave about two inches of margin at the top of each page and about an inch at the bottom to facilitate editing.
11. Always circle in pencil everything that is *NOT* to be read on the air. This would include slug-lines and notations at the bottom of the page.
12. Do not use newspaper copy-editing symbols to correct mistakes. If you make an error in a word, do not erase, simply X through it and type it again.
13. If your copy gets too difficult to read because of errors, it might be better to retype it rather than confuse the announcer by a myriad of arrows, X's and other symbols.

ABBREVIATIONS

1. Do not use abbreviations unless you want them read as abbreviations.
2. Exceptions include such titles as Dr., Mrs., and Mr. The same is true of certain cities such as St. Louis, St. Paul, and the like. All of these are so commonly used that there is no problem of confusion.
3. Abbreviate the names of groups, organizations and governmental agencies only when their titles are commonly used. For example, F-B-I, Y-M-C-A, N-A-A-C-P, etc. are commonly used so they do not require elaboration. But when you have an unusual abbreviation, it is essential that you give its full title the first time:

    POOR: The F-A-A will meet this afternoon to rule on the matter.
    BETTER: The Federal Aviation Agency—the F-A-A- will meet this afternoon. . . .

4. Always use hyphens between letters you want read as letters—never periods. If you want the letters read as a word (UNESCO, NATO, CORE, NASA, etc.), then leave out the hyphens.
5. Only abbreviate United States when using it as an adjective. Otherwise, write it out.

    The president pledged a steady supply of U-S aid.
    The United States will provide aid.

6. When in doubt about an abbreviation, spell it out.

NAMES AND TITLES

1. Do not begin a story with an unfamiliar name. Delay it until you have the listener's attention:

> POOR: Monte Briar, state chairman for the Easter Seals campaign, was killed in an auto accident today.
> BETTER: The state chairman for the Easter Seals campaign was killed in an auto accident today. Monte Briar died when his car. . . .

2. Titles are preferred before the name to parallel common speaking habits.
3. Avoid using long titles. If it is long, break it up.

> POOR: Senate Foreign Relations Committee Attorney Tom Smith
> BETTER: Attorney Tom Smith of the Senate Foreign Relations Committee

4. Radio-TV style prefers that middle initials and names be omitted unless they are widely recognized as part of the name. For example, it is proper to write: Henry Cabot Lodge, John L. Lewis, George Bernard Shaw, etc.
5. Use the full name in the first mention, but afterwards the last name is sufficient. For example: Robert Jones was arrested today. Jones was charged with. . . .
6. Never refer to the president of the United States by just his last name. Always call him Mr. or President:

> POOR: Reagan spoke to the group today. He said. . . .
> BETTER: The president spoke to the group today. Mr. Reagan said. . . .

7. Use Mr. and Mrs. when referring to a husband and wife together.
8. Do not use Mr. when referring to a man's name standing alone.

> Mr. and Mrs. William Smith were informed last night that their son was one of ten soldiers who died in yesterday's helicopter crash. Mrs. Smith was placed under a doctor's care immediately. Smith plans to go to San Francisco to attend funeral services.

9. Members of the clergy are also an exception to the rule about using names standing alone. Always use a title when referring to a clergyman:

Protestant:
> First reference—The Reverend Mr. John Brown
> Second reference—The Reverend Mr. Brown

Catholic:
> First reference—The Reverend John Brown
> Second reference—Father (or Bishop or Cardinal) Brown

Jewish:
>First reference—Rabbi Martin London
>Second reference—Rabbi London

PRONUNCIATION

1. When the pronunciation of a word is in doubt, it is your obligation to provide the proper form. This may be done by providing phonetic spelling of the word after the troublesome term *each time* it is used. There are three techniques you can use depending on your news director's preference:
a) After the word:
>The junta (h-un-ta) was overthrown.
b) Over the word:
>   (h-un-ta)
>The junta was overthrown.
c) In place of the word:
>The h-un-ta was overthrown.
It is not essential that you use the ''correct'' phonetic spelling. You may use any combination of letters you wish as long as the announcer can understand. But keep it simple.

PUNCTUATION

1. The listener cannot see punctuation marks. They are only to help the announcer interpret the copy. Don't use them except where they are absolutely essential for the announcer.
2. *Do not* use the following marks. They are confusing and meaningless in radio-TV news:

>   : ; ( ) & % $@ c ½ ¼

3. Generally you should restrict your punctuation to commas, periods, question marks, quotation marks, and dots and dashes.
4. Dashes (—) or dots (. . .) are used to indicate longer pauses or parenthetical matter.

>   Tom Zeigle . . . well-known local educator . . . has gone to the state capitol to seek—what he calls—a redress of grievances.

5. Hyphens are used to indicate that letters are to be read individually (N-A-T-O).
6. The hyphen is used when a name is to be spelled out (J-o-n-e-s).
7. The hyphen is used when a telephone number or address is to be spelled out (Highland 6-7-8-0-9).

PRONOUNS

1. Be careful about using pronouns. Make sure they agree with their antecedent in both gender and number. Groups, organizations and companies are singular, and therefore take the singular form of the verb and pronoun.

> POOR: The city council voted no. *They* passed. . . .
> BETTER: The city council voted no. *It* passed. . . .

2. Make sure the listener can clearly understand to what the pronoun refers.

> POOR: Police tonight charged John Warren with drunk driving after an accident involving his car and one driven by Walter Joseph. Police say *he* veered. . . . (Does "he" refer to Warren or Joseph?)
> BETTER: Police tonight charged John Warren. . . . Police say *Warren's* car veered. . . .

3. The pronoun *that* is a weak word. Eliminate as many as possible. The best way to decide whether you can leave *that* out is to read the sentence out aloud with and without the word and see if it still *flows*.

> POOR: He said *that* it is important *that* we understand *that* the college can't. . . .
> BETTER: He said it is important we understand the college can't. . . .

NUMBERS

There are two basic problems in the use of numbers in broadcast news:
) How do we write the numbers so as not to confuse the announcer?
) How do we present the numbers so as not to confuse the audience?

Announcer

1. For numbers one through nine, write them out.
2. For numbers 10 through 999, use figures except for eleven which is written out.
3. For numbers above 999, use a combination of numbers and spelling. This avoids strings of numbers which can be confusing.

> 987,098 would be written 987-thousand and -98
> 11,000 would be written eleven thousand (remember to write out eleven)
> 6,780,000 would be written six million-780-thousand
> 1,400 would be written 14-hundred

4. Write "one thousand" rather than "a thousand." "A" can sound like "eight."

5. Use figures for all ages. And the age *precedes* the name, as in "13-year old Regio Jacks."
6. Use figures for all dates and addresses (June 2nd, 3rd Avenue).
7. Write out fractions: one-half, one-fourth rather than ½, ¼, etc.
8. Write out "per cent" rather than using "%."
9. Write out dollar and cents rather than using "$" and "c."
10. Always write out a number if it begins a sentence.
11. In decimals, spell out decimal point (two point nine per cent).

Audience

1. Rarely are precise statistics necessary to grasp the significance of a story. Therefore, it is acceptable to round off numbers.

   > POOR: The budget calls for 6,456 dollars for education.
   > BETTER: The budget calls for just under 65-hundred dollars for education.

2. When you round off figures, use terms like *just over, about, close to,* etc.
3. Avoid long lists of numbers. The listener won't understand them all anyway.
4. When using large numbers, be creative in finding some way of relating the figure in meaningful terms your audience will appreciate.

   > POOR: The defense budget has been set at 500 million dollars.
   > BETTER: The defense budget has been set at 500 million dollars, or two and a half dollars for every man, woman and child in America.

5. In writing time, use figures. Don't use A.M. and P.M., instead use "this morning," "tomorrow night," "this afternoon," etc.
6. Unless the exact time is necessary (which is almost never), avoid mentioning it. Instead be general:

   > early this evening
   > late tonight
   > late last night
   > early this morning
   > about an hour ago
   > in about two hours

7. Avoid the term *per,* as in "miles per hour" or "cents per pound." Write it "cents a pound" or "miles an hour."

QUOTATIONS

1. Since it is impossible for the audience to "see" the quotation marks, it is left to the writer and the announcer to tell the audience in some fashion that the material is a direct quote.
2. You can indicate direct quotes by having the announcer change inflection.

3. You can avoid the problem by re-phrasing direct quotes into indirect statements.

4. Avoid the use of "quote-unquote." This is awkward. Instead, use phrases such as the following to indicate a direct quotation:

> —We quote her exact words. . . .
> —In his words. . . .
> —As she put it. . . .
> —The statement read in part. . . .
> —What he called (or termed, or described as). . . .

5. Avoid lengthy quotes when possible. But if you have to use them, break them up by inserting such phrases as *he went on to say, he added, he continued,* etc.

EDITING COPY FOR THE AIR

1. Although it is assumed that you have been reading your copy as you prepare each story, it is essential that you completely reread the copy for errors, potential libel, grammar, taste, etc., after it is finished.

2. Never use newspaper editing symbols when correcting broadcast copy.

3. If you have to make major alterations in your copy, it is better that you retype the entire story rather than creating a confusing mass of corrections.

4. If minor corrections are to be made, simply black out the error completely and write the correction above the error (this is the reason for triple spacing).

MISCELLANEOUS

1. Radio and TV writing is relatively informal. Use contractions (don't, isn't) wherever possible except where you want to emphasize the negative aspect.

2. Avoid obscure, non-local names in your stories. When the names are of no significance to *your* audience, rewrite the story to eliminate them.

> POOR: A family of seven was killed late today in a two-car accident in Los Angeles, California. Dead is 44-year old Rod Taylor, his wife 38-year-old Mary and their five children, 14-year-old Rod junior, 13-year-old Melissa, 10-year old Linda, 8-year-old Robert, and 5-year-old Timothy, all of Tarzana, California.
> BETTER: Seven persons . . . all members of a Tarzana, California family . . . were killed late today in a two-car accident in Los Angeles, California. The head-on collision took the lives of a father, mother, and their five children, ranging in age from five to 14.

3. On the other hand, names of persons from your listening area are always important regardless of where the story originates. It is essential that you scan stories—especially disaster items—for local names and play them close to the lead.

4. In disaster stories, if no local people are involved say so.
5. Identify obscure geographical areas in relation to places which are well known to your listeners.

> POOR: The tornado caused extensive damage to Paradise, California
> BETTER: The tornado caused extensive damage to Paradise, Californi
> . . . a small foothill community some 200 miles north of San Francisco

6. When dealing with subject matter which has a specialized jargon or nomen clature, translate these terms into words and concepts easily understood b the average listener.

> POOR: The Apollo launch was aborted due to insufficient pressure in liquid oxygen transmission system.
> BETTER: The Apollo launch was called off because of a blocked fue line which carries liquid oxygen.

7. When referring to groups, organizations, governing bodies, etc. which ma not be well known to the general public, it is essential that you tell your lis tener what the group does.

> POOR: Pickets appeared this morning at the annual Sigma Delta Ch convention in San Diego. . . .
> BETTER: Pickets appeared this morning at the Sigma Delta Chi con vention in San Diego. . . . Sigma Delta Chi is the national honorary so ciety of journalists.

FINAL STEPS

Before you turn your copy over to your editor, you should run through the fol lowing checklist:

1. Copyread and edit for accuracy, good taste, libel, grammar, spell ing, etc.
2. Make sure no words are split between lines.
3. Make sure no sentences are split between pages.
4. Make sure everything that is not to be read on the air is circled with pencil.
5. Double-check order of pages in your story.
6. Make sure each page ends with either an end mark (### or—30 or "MORE."
7. Write total line count of story (15 lines of radio copy equals one minute) on top of first page and circle it.

APPENDIX B
Common Writing Errors

If you paid close attention to the guidelines, your writing should be clear, concise, and will meet the requirements of broadcast style. However, there are some common mistakes that many experienced writers commit without even thinking. UPI suggests you be aware of the following common faults:

1. He *dived* into the water, not *dove*.
2. *Character* is what one really possesses; *reputation* is what one is supposed to have.
3. *Farther* refers to distance. *Further* means more or additional.
4. Not all *real estate sellers* are *realtors*. A *realtor* is a member of a local real estate board having membership in the National Association of Real Estate Boards.
5. *Murder* is the technical term denoting a degree of guilt and should be used carefully.
6. *It's* is the contraction for *it is*. *Its* is the possessive form of *it*.
7. *Heart disease* is an ailment of the heart, not the cause of death, which is *heart failure*.
8. A *scholar* is a learned person. A child in school is only a *pupil* or *student*.
9. *Affect* and *effect* don't mean the same thing.
10. It is *proved*, not *proven*.
11. A person dies *of* a disease, not *from* a disease.
12. *Rosary* is *recited* or said. A *Mass* is *celebrated*.
13. She is the *widow* of her husband, not her *late* husband. He leaves *his widow* not *his wife*.

14. *Who* refers to persons; *which* to animals, things, or ideas. *That* refers to persons, animals, things, or ideas. Don't say the persons which.
15. Fifty *persons,* not fifty *people.* But the *people* of a country or city is correct.
16. A *sum of money* takes a singular verb. Ten cents is correct English.
17. *Suicide* is a *noun,* it cannot be used as a verb.
18. A turkey is *red-headed,* not a girl who is *red-haired.*
19. Something is unique, perfect, round, certain, and other absolute terms. To add modifiers such as very, most, nearly, more, less, etc. is incorrect.
20. A prisoner is *hanged,* not *hung.*
21. Don't say a person broke his arm unless he did so on purpose.
22. Attendance is more than 100, not over 100.
23. *Injured* refers only to living things; *damage* refers to objects.
24. There is a difference between *house* and *home.* A *home* is not sold. A *house* is.
25. A child is *reared.* Chickens are *raised.*

No matter what the viewpoint regarding definitions, there can be no disagreement that words should be used to convey the meaning intended by their employers. Caution, therefore, is advisable in deviating from original usages.

The following are some words and expressions which often cause difficulty:

ABOVE: Should not be used for *over* or *more than.*
ACCORD: Do not use in the sense of *award. Give* is better.
ACT: A single incident. An *action* consists of several acts.
ADMINISTER: Used with reference to medicine, governments or oaths. Blows are not *administered,* but *dealt.*
ADOPT: Not synonymous with *decide* or *assume.*
AFFECT; EFFECT: *Affect* means to have an influence on; *Effect* means to cause, to produce, to result in.
AGGRAVATE: Means to *increase;* not synonymous with *irritate.*
ALLEGE: Not synonymous with *assert.* Say the *alleged* crime, but "He said he is innocent."
ALLOW; PERMIT: The former means *not to forbid;* the latter means *to grant leave.*
ALLUDE: Do not confuse with *refer.*
ALMOST; NEARLY: *Almost* regards the ending of an act; *nearly* the beginning.
ALTERNATIVE: Indicates a choice of two things. It is incorrect to speak of *two alternatives* or *one alternative.*
AMONG: Use when more than two is meant; for two only use *between.*
ANTECEDENTS: Do not use in the sense of *ancestors, forefathers, history* or *origin.*
A NUMBER OF: Indefinite. Specify.

ANXIOUS: Implies worry. Not synonymous with *eager* which implies anticipation or desire.

ANYONE OR NONE: Use in speaking of more than two. *Either* and *neither* are used when speaking of only two. All take singular verbs.

APPEARS, LOOKS, SMELLS, SEEMS, ETC.: Takes an adjective complement.

AS THE RESULT OF AN OPERATION: Avoid this expression. Usually incorrect and libelous.

AT: Use *in* before names of large cities: He is *in* New York, but the meeting was held *at* Greenville.

AUDIENCE: An *audience* hears, *spectators* see.

AUTOPSY: An *autopsy* is *performed,* not *held.*

AVOCATION: A man's pleasure, while *vocation* is his business or profession.

AWFUL: Means *to fill with awe;* not synonymous with *very* or *extremely.*

BALANCE: Not synonymous with *rest* or *remainder.*

BANQUET: Only a few dinners are worth the name. Use *dinner* or *supper.*

BECAUSE: Better than *due to* in, "They fought because of a misunderstanding."

BESIDE; BESIDES: The first means *by the side of;* the second, *in addition to.*

BY: Use instead of *with* in such sentences as, "The effect was gained by colored lights."

CALL ATTENTION: Do not use it for *direct attention.*

CANON; CANNON: The former is a *law;* the latter is a large *gun.*

CANVAS; CANVASS: The former is a *cloth;* the latter means *to solicit.*

CAPITOL: The building is the *Capitol;* the city is the *capital.*

CASUALTY: Should not be confused with *disaster, accident, mishap.*

CHILDISH: Not synonymous with *childlike.*

CHINESE: Don't use *Chinaman.*

CLAIM: A transitive verb. One may "claim a dog" but not that "Boston is larger than Portland."

COLD FACTS (or statistics): When is a fact hot?

COLLIDE: To collide both objects must be in motion.

COMMENCE: Usually *begin* or *start* is better.

COMPARED WITH: Use *compared with* in speaking of two things coming under the same classification; use *compared to* if the classes are different.

COMPLETELY DESTROYED: Redundant.

COMPRISE: Do not use for *compose.*

CONFESS: A man confesses a crime to the police, but he does not confess to a crime.

CONSCIOUS: Not synonymous with *aware.*

CONSENSUS: Don't say *consensus of opinion;* simply say *consensus.*

CONSEQUENCE: Sometimes misused in the sense of *importance* and *of moment,* as "They are all persons of consequence" (importance) "A matter of no consequence" (moment).

CONSISTS IN: Distinguish between *consists in* and *consists of.*

CONSUMMATION: Look up in the dictionary. Do not use in reference to marriage.

CONTINUAL; CONTINUOUS: That is -al which either is always going on or recurs at short intervals and never comes (or is regarded as never coming) to an end. That is -ous in which no break occurs between the beginning and the end.

CONVENE: Delegates, not a convention, convene.

CORRESPONDENT; CO-RESPONDENT: The former communicates in writing; the latter answers jointly with another.

COUNCIL; COUNSEL: The former is a meeting for deliberation. The latter is advice or one who gives advice.

COUPLE: Used only when two things are joined, not of separate things.

CRIME: Do not confuse with *sin* or *vice. Crime* is a violation of the law of the state; *vice* refers to a violation of moral law; *sin* is a violation of religious law.

CULTURED: Don't use for *cultivated.*

CYCLONE: Distinguish from *hurricane, typhoon, tornado, gale,* and *storm.*

DANGEROUSLY: Not *dangerously* but *critically* or *alarmingly ill.*

DATA: Plural. *Datum* is singular.

DATE FROM: Not *date back to.*

DEPOT: Don't use for *station.* A *depot* is a storehouse for freight or supplies; railway passengers arrive at a *station.*

DIFFERENT FROM: Not *different than.*

DIMENSIONS; PROPORTIONS: The former pertains to magnitude; the latter to form.

DIVIDE: Don't say, "The money was divided between Smith, Jones, and Brown." Use *among* when more than two are concerned.

DOVE: Should not be used for *dived.*

DROPS DEAD: *Falls dead* is what is meant.

DURING: Do not confuse with *in. During* answers the question, "How long?" *In* the question, "What?" "At what time?" as, "We were in Princeton during the winter."; "We received the letter *in* the morning."

EACH OTHER; ONE ANOTHER: The former pertains to two; the latter to three or more.

EITHER; NEITHER: Use when speaking of two only.

ELICIT: Means to *draw out against the will.*

EMIGRANT: Do not confuse with *immigrant.* An *emigrant* leaves, and an *immigrant* comes in.

ENVELOP; ENVELOPE: The former means to *surround;* the latter is a covering or wrapper.

EVENT: Do not confuse with *incident, affair, occurrence,* or *happening.*

EXPERIMENT: Don't say *try* an experiment. Experiments are *made.*

FAIL: To *fail* one must try. Usually what is meant is *did not.*

FAKIR; FAKER: The former is an Oriental ascetic; the latter is a street peddler.

FARTHER: Denotes distance; *further* denotes time.

FINAL; FINALE: The former means *last;* the latter is a concluding act or number.

FRANKENSTEIN: In the story he was the monster's maker, not the monster itself.

FROM: A person dies *of,* not *from,* a disease.

GRADUATE, as a verb: Colleges *graduate;* students *are graduated.*

GUN: Don't confuse with *revolver* and *pistol.*

HAD: Implies volition. Don't say, "had his arm cut off."

HEALTHY: A person is *healthy,* but climate is *healthful* and food *wholesome.*

HEART FAILURE: Everyone dies of *heart failure.* There are several *heart diseases.*

HECTIC: "Hectic flush" is the feverish blush of consumption. Not to be used in the sense of *excited, impassioned, intense, rapturous, uncontrolled,* or *wild,* except when a jocosity is intended.

HIGH: Distinguish from *large.*

HOI POLLOI: "The many." Do not use "the" before it.

HOLD: Use advisedly. The Supreme Court *holds* a law constitutional, but one *asserts* that one man is a better boxer than another.

HUNG: A criminal is *hanged.* Clothes are *hung* on a line.

INAUGURATE: Does not mean *begin.*

INCUMBENT: It is redundant to write *present incumbent.*

INDORSE: Not synonymous with *approve.*

INFER; IMPLY: The former means to *deduce;* the latter to *signify.*

INITIAL: A man may sign his initial, but he does not make an *initial payment.* He makes the *first payment.*

INNUMERABLE: Not synonymous with *endless.*

INVITED GUESTS: Most guests are invited; omit the adjective.

LAST: Not synonymous with *latest* or *past.*

LEAVE: Don't confuse with *let.*

LEAVES A WIDOW: Impossible. He leaves a *wife.*

LESS: Use *less* money but *fewer* coins.

LIKE: The slogan, "Winstons taste good like a cigaret should," has helped make the use of *like* legitimate as a substitute for *as.*

LITERALLY: Often the exact opposite, *figuratively,* is meant.

LOCATE: A building is *located* when its site is picked; thereafter it is *situated.* A person is *found,* not located.

MAJORITY: The lead over *all* others; a plurality is a lead over *one* other.

MATHEMATICS: Singular.

MEMORANDUM: Singular. *Memoranda,* plural.

MEND: You *mend* a dress but *repair* a street.

MINISTER: Distinguish between *minister,* a term used in Protestant chur ches, and *priest,* used in Catholic churches. Every *preacher* is not *pastor;* a *pastor* has a church, a *minister* may not.

MUSICAL; MUSICALE: The former means *rhythmic;* the latter is a *reci tal* or *concert.*

NAME AFTER: The correct form is *name for.*

NEAR ACCIDENT: There is no such thing.

NEE: Give only last name, "Mrs. Helen Kuenzel, nee Bauman."

NICE: Means *exact,* not *agreeable* or *pleasant.*

NOTORIOUS: Different from *famous.*

OCCUR: Accidents *occur* rather than *happen,* but weddings *take place.*

OLD ADAGES: There are no new adages.

OVER: Means *above; more than* means *in excess of.*

PARTLY COMPLETED: Has no meaning. The words are contradictory.

PAST: Not synonymous with *last.*

PEOPLE: Refers to population. Do not confuse with *persons.*

PER CENT: Do not say *large per cent* when you mean *large proportion.*

POLITICS: Singular.

PRACTICALLY: Not synonymous with *virtually.* Different from *almost.*

PRINCIPLE: Always a noun. *Principal* is generally an adjective.

PRONE ON THE BACK: Impossible. The word means *lying on the face Supine is lying on the back.*

PROVIDED: Not *providing* he will go.

PUBLIC: Singular.

PUT IN: You *occupy, devote,* or *spend* time, never *put in* time.

QUITE: Means *fully* or *wholly.* Do not, for example, write, "He is *quite* wealthy," but, "He is *rather* wealthy."

RAISED: Animals are *raised;* children are *reared.*

RENDER: You *render* lard or a judgment, but you *sing* a song.

RUMOR: It is redundant to write *unverified rumor.*

SECURE: Means *to make fast.* Don't use it for *obtain, procure,* or *ac quire.*

SENSATION; EMOTION: The former is physical; the latter is mental.

SHIP: Cattle are *shipped* but corpses are *sent.*

SO: Use in a negative comparison instead of *as.*

SOMEONE, SOMEBODY, ETC.: Take singular verbs.

SUICIDE: Do not use as a verb.

SUSTAIN: Injuries are not *sustained* but *received.*

TO THE NTH: An unspecified number, not necessarily infinite or large Do not use for *to the utmost possible extent.*

TRANSPIRE: Means to *emerge from secrecy into knowledge, to become gradually known.* Not to be used in the senses of *happen, occur* etc.; must not be followed by an infinitive.

TREBLE; TRIPLE: The former means three times; the latter means three kinds.

TRUE FACTS: Facts never are false.

TRY AND: Use *try to.*

UNIQUE: Its adverbs are *absolutely, almost, in some respects, nearly, perhaps, quite, really,* and *surely.* It does not admit of comparison. There are no degrees of uniqueness. It means *alone of its kind. Different* means *out of the ordinary.*

UNKNOWN, UNIDENTIFIED: The former means *not recognizable by anyone;* the latter means *not yet recognized.*

VARIOUS: Not synonymous with *different.*

WANT; WISH: The former means *need* and *desire;* the latter means only *desire.*

WELL-KNOWN: Usually *widely known* is meant.

WHETHER: Do not use for *if.* Don't add *or not.*

WIDOW: Never use *widow woman.*

YACHT: Do not say *private yacht.* There are no *public* ones.

The one thing that marks a beginning reporter is verbosity—using flowery language when simple, more direct terms would do the same thing. The following are some of the more common pitfalls:

1. SEND something—don't transmit or dispatch it.
2. CALL a person to a meeting—don't summon him.
3. BUY something—don't purchase it.
4. LEAVE—don't depart.
5. ACT—don't take action.
6. TRY—don't always attempt.
7. ARREST—not take into custody.
8. SHOW—don't always display or exhibit.
9. HELP—not always aid or assist.
10. BECAUSE—not always due to the fact that.
11. NEED—don't always require.

The beginning writer should always be aware of clichés and should try to avoid using them in his stories. An excellent observation on the overuse of some phrases was written by a Scandinavian immigrant, Hugo Johanson and printed by *Atlantic Monthly* in 1946:

Soon, I could make out that, by and large, the republic's divorcees were gay, the bachelors confirmed, the matrons comely, the men self-made, the pies home-made, the lies fabricated, the students gifted, the gamblers notorious, the chefs famous, the authors and lecturers noted, the recluses wealthy, the white trash poor, the travelers intrepid, the diplomats distinguished, the hold-up men desperate, the lawyers astute, the politicians slick, the statesmen august, the businessmen successful, the octogenarians spry, the cows contented, the masses seething, the physicians prominent the singers captivating, the prospectors grizzled, the rumors ugly, the con fessions true, the stories short, the tales tall, the hopes high, the front false, and the bootleggers alleged.

APPENDIX C
AP Wire Copy

The best way to understand how the news wires operate is to take a look at a brief portion of the Associated Press wire which "moved" from 9:55 a.m. till 1:55 p.m. on April 9, 1986. Explanations of various symbols, abbreviations, etc., are included *in italics*. The copy was obtained from the Los Angeles bureau of AP. Depending on your location, you would get your news from the closest regional and state bureaus during the national split.

B161 [*Each story has its own "book" number which serves as a reference point.*]
   RD
AP-13TH NEWSWATCH
[*Sent at regular intervals throughout a twenty-four hour cycle. The newswatch gives a self-contained five minute national and international newscast.*]

HERE IS THE LATEST NEWS FROM THE ASSOCIATED PRESS:
   LIBYAN LEADER MOAMMAR KHADAFY (MOO'-AH-MAHR KAH-DAH'-FEE) SOUNDS READY FOR A FIGHT. SPEAKING TO REPORT-ERS IN HIS HEAVILY-GUARDED TRIPOLI BUNKER, KHADAFY HAS DECLARED THAT MILITARY PLANS ARE COMPLETE TO CHAL-LENGE THE UNITED STATES. KHADAFY VOWED TO STEP-UP VIO-LENCE AGAINST AMERICAN TARGETS, CIVILIAN AND NON-CIVIL-IAN—WORLDWIDE. WEARING A GREEN UNIFORM AND BLACK BERET, KHADAFY TOLD REPORTERS "AMERICA WILL BE DE-FEATED MILITARILY."
   KHADAFY SAID HE WAS RESPONDING TO THE LATEST AMERI-CAN THREATS AGAINST LIBYA. YESTERDAY, A SENIOR U-S OFFI-CIAL SAID THE REAGAN ADMINISTRATION HAS DECIDED THE U-S

WILL RETALIATE AGAINST LIBYA, BUT THE TARGET AND TIMING
HAVE NOT BEEN DETERMINED.

VICE PRESIDENT GEORGE BUSH HAS ADDED HIS VOICE TO THE
RISING RHETORIC. ADDRESSING SAILORS ABOARD THE U-S-S "EN-
TERPRISE" IN THE GULF OF OMAN, BUSH CALLED KHADAFY A
"MAD DOG" WHO'S BEEN TAUGHT A LESSON BY U-S MILITARY
STRIKES IN THE GULF OF SIDRA (SIH'-DRUH). BUSH FLEW TO THE
AIRCRAFT CARRIER AS IT STEAMED THROUGH SHIPPING LANES IN
THE MIDDLE EAST.

WEST GERMANY IS EXPELLING TWO LIBYAN DIPLOMATS. BUT
WEST GERMAN OFFICIALS HAVE REVERSED AN EARLIER STATE-
MENT AND NOW SAY THE EXPULSION IS NOT DIRECTLY LINKED
TO THE WEEKEND BOMBING OF A NIGHTCLUB WHICH KILLED A
U-S SERVICEMAN. WEST GERMANY SAYS THE TWO LIBYANS HAD
BEEN UNDER SURVEILLANCE FOR SOME TIME.

A MEMORIAL SERVICE FOR THREE AMERICAN VICTIMS OF TER-
RORISM WAS HELD TODAY IN ATHENS. THE SERVICE WAS FOR DE-
METRA STYLIAN, HER DAUGHTER AND EIGHT MONTH OLD
GRANDCHILD OF ANNAPOLIS, MARYLAND. THE THREE AND A
CONNECTICUT MAN WERE KILLED WHEN A BOMB BLEW UP
ABOARD A T-W-A JETLINER APRIL SECOND. ALL FOUR BODIES ARE
EXPECTED TO BE RETURNED TO THE U-S LATER THIS WEEK.

AN OFFICIAL OF THE INTERNATIONAL FEDERATION OF AIRLINE
PILOTS ASSOCIATIONS SAYS THERE'S EVIDENCE THE CRASH OF A
MEXICANA AIRLINES JET LAST MONDAY WAS NO ACCIDENT. THE
727 JET SLAMMED INTO A MOUNTAIN, KILLING ALL 166 PEOPLE
ABOARD. PILOTS ASSOCIATION PRESIDENT REG SMITH SAYS
THERE'S EVIDENCE AN EXPLOSION OCCURRED DURING THE BRIEF
FLIGHT, "PROBABLY CAUSED BY A BOMB."

FORMER U-N SECRETARY-GENERAL KURT WALDHEIM SAYS HE
WON'T QUIT HIS RUN FOR THE PRESIDENCY OF AUSTRIA DESPITE
ALLEGATIONS THAT HE'S HIDING FROM A NAZI PAST. WALDHEIM
HAS TOLD A WEST GERMAN NEWSPAPER HE WON'T BOW OUT OF
THE RACE. THE FORMER U-N OFFICIAL REPEATED HIS DENIALS
THAT HE EVER WAS A NAZI.

POLICE IN ITALY CONTINUE A NATIONWIDE ROUND-UP OF
TAINTED WINE THAT HAS KILLED 20 PEOPLE. AUTHORITIES SAY
THE LOW BUDGET WINE IS POISONED WITH METHYL ALCOHOL
THAT WAS USED ILLEGALLY TO RAISE THE WINE'S ALCOHOL
CONTENT. THE VATICAN HAS ASSURED ROMAN CATHOLICS THE
TAINTED WINE IS NOT THE SAME WINE USED DURING MASS.

NEWSWATCH BY RICHARD ULIANO

AP-LA-04-09-86 0953 T

[*The slugline at the end of each AP story indicates the time and date the item
was transmitted. The originating bureau is indicated by a one or two letter code*

before the date. Then the time for the end of each transmission is shown to allow clients to recognize the latest information.]
B162

UO

AP-(NORCAL RECREATIONAL FORECAST)

[*Each of the wire services provides customized weather reports for clients in various parts of the country and the world.*]

MONTEREY BAY RECREATIONAL FORECAST, SANTA CRUZ TO MONTEREY INCLUDING THE BAY WATERS . . . SUNNY TODAY EXCEPT FOR PATCHY MORNING FOG OR LOW CLOUDS. HIGHS IN THE MID 60S TO LOW 70S. FAIR TONIGHT EXCEPT FOR PATCHY LATE NIGHT FOG. LOWS IN THE 40S. SUNNY TOMORROW EXCEPT FOR PATCHY MORNING FOG. HIGHS IN THE MID 60S TO LOW 70S. MONTEREY, 68/47 AND SANTA CRUZ, 66/46.

BOATERS FORECAST FOR MONTEREY BAY . . . WIND NORTHWEST 5 TO 15 KNOTS. OCCASIONALLY TO 20 KNOTS THIS AFTERNOON THROUGH TOMORROW. COMBINED SEAS 3 TO 5 FEET.

AP-LA-04-09-86 0955 T

B163

UB

AP-EBS BULLETIN TEST

[*Required of all broadcast stations and the press services.*]

XXXXXXXXXXXXXXXXXXXXXXXXXXXXXXXXXXXXXXXXXXXXXXXXX

THIS IS A TEST OF THE EMERGENCY ACTION NOTIFICATION SYSTEM.

IF THIS WERE NOT A TEST, YOU WOULD RECEIVE AN AUTHENTICATOR WORD, AN EMERGENCY ACTION NOTIFICATION MESSAGE, AND THE SAME AUTHENTICATOR WORD AGAIN.

THIS IS A TEST OF THE EMERGENCY ACTION NOTIFICATION SYSTEM.

ALL STATIONS SHOULD FOLLOW PROCEDURES ON THEIR EBS CHECKLISTS FOR TELETYPE TESTS.

XXXXXXXXXXXXXXXXXXXXXXXXXXXXXXXXXXXXXXXXXXXXXXXXX

AP-LA-04-09-86 0956 T

B164

UO

AP-(NORCAL COASTAL FORECAST)

POINT ST GEORGE TO POINT ARENA OUT 60 MILES—WIND NORTH 5 TO 15 KNOTS WAVES 1 TO 3 FEET BECOMING NORTH 10 TO 20 KNOTS WAVES 2 TO 4 FEET TOMORROW. SWELL NORTHWEST 5 TO 7 FEET PATCHY FOG AND LOW CLOUDS INCREASING TONIGHT AND TOMORROW.

POINT ARENA TO POINT PINOS OUT 60 MILES—WIND NORTH-

WEST 5 TO 15 KNOTS EXCEPT OCCASIONALLY 20 KTS AFTER-
NOONS. WAVES 1 TO 3 FEET. SWELL NORTHWEST 3 TO 5 FEET.
PATCHY NIGHT AND MORNING FOG OR LOW CLOUDS INCREASING
TONIGHT AND TOMORROW.

POINT PINOS TO POINT CONCEPTION OUT 60 MILES—WIND
NORTHWEST INCREASING TO 10 TO 20 KNOTS AFTERNOONS
THROUGH TOMORROW. WAVES 2 TO 4 FEET. SWELL NORTHWEST 3
TO 5 FEET. PATCHY NIGHT AND MORNING FOG OR LOW CLOUDS
OTHERWISE FAIR.

SAN FRANCISCO, SAN PABLO, SUISUN BAYS WEST DELTA—
WIND VARIABLE 5 TO 15 BECOMING WESTERLY TO 20 KNOTS
AFTERNOONS AND EVENINGS THROUGH TOMORROW. FAIR TO-
DAY. INCREASING LOW CLOUDS OR PATCHY FOG TONIGHT AND
EARLY TOMORROW MORNING. FAIR TOMORROW AFTERNOON.

     AP-LA-04-09-86 0959 T

B165

   UF

AP-BUSINESSWATCH

[*One of many specialized features provided by AP during the regular broadcast
cycle.*]

   DOLLAR-GOLD (TOPS)

   (LONDON)—THE U-S DOLLAR FELL TODAY AGAINST ALL KEY
CURRENCIES EXCEPT THE BRITISH POUND IN HECTIC EUROPEAN
TRADING, AMID SPECULATION THAT THE BIG FIVE WESTERN IN-
DUSTRIALIZED NATIONS ARE PLANNING ADDITIONAL CUTS IN IN-
TEREST RATES.

BUT CURRENCY DEALERS SAY THE DOLLAR RALLIED SLIGHTLY
IN LATE TRADING AFTER WEST GERMAN OFFICIALS—WHO AT-
TENDED YESTERDAY'S GROUP OF FIVE MEETING IN WASHING-
TON—INDICATED THAT THE FINANCE MINISTERS AND CENTRAL
BANK OFFICIALS HAD NOT DISCUSSED THE POSSIBLE NEED TO
FURTHER WEAKEN THE DOLLAR.

THE FIVE NATIONS AGREED LAST SEPTEMBER ON CONCERTED
ACTION TO LOWER THE DOLLAR IN A BID TO PUSH DOWN INTER-
EST RATES WORLDWIDE AND REDUCE THE UNITED STATES' MAS-
SIVE TRADE DEFICIT.

EARLIER, A TOKYO NEWSPAPER REPORTED THAT THE BANK OF
JAPAN PLANS TO LOWER ITS DISCOUNT RATE—THE INTEREST
RATE IT CHARGES ON LOANS TO COMMERCIAL BANKS.

THE PRICE OF GOLD CLOSED TODAY IN LONDON AT 337 DOL-
LARS AN OUNCE—DOWN 50 CENTS FROM YESTERDAY. THE ZU-
RICH CLOSE WAS 337 DOLLARS AND 50 CENTS—A LOSS OF THREE
DOLLARS AN OUNCE.

     AP-LA-04-09-86 1002 T

166
UB
AP-URGENT-REAGAN-LIBYA
(WASHINGTON)—PRESIDENT REAGAN SAYS THE UNITED STATES
WON'T JUST "SIT HERE AND HOLD STILL," AS HE PUT IT, IN THE
WAKE OF NEW TERRORIST ATTACKS AGAINST AMERICANS IN EU-
ROPE.
THE PRESIDENT SAID TODAY THAT LIBYAN LEADER KHADAFY
IS "DEFINITELY A SUSPECT" IN THE LATEST FATAL BOMBINGS ON
A T-W-A JETLINER AND A WEST BERLIN NIGHTCLUB.
SPEAKING TO A GROUP OF NEWSPAPER EDITORS IN WASHING-
TON, REAGAN REFUSED TO SAY WHAT HE PLANS TO DO IN RE-
SPONSE TO THE TERRORIST INCIDENTS. BUT THE PRESIDENT SAID
HIS ADMINISTRATION WOULD CONTINUE TO GATHER EVIDENCE—
AND SEEK THE SUPPORT OF EUROPEAN ALLIES.
WITH ADDITIONAL EVIDENCE, REAGAN SAID, THE U-S WOULD
BE ABLE TO "POINT A FINGER AT WHO IS RESPONSIBLE."
WHEN ASKED IF THE EVIDENCE NOW POINTS TO KHADAFY, THE
PRESIDENT RESPONDED, "LET ME SAY HE IS DEFINITELY A SUS-
PECT."
        AP-LA-04-09-86 1005 T
167
UN
NY27
UNBX PD99 PD30
UNBX
AP-(SULLY TRIAL)
(SAN MATEO)—FORMER POLICEMAN ANTHONY "JACK" SULLY
WAS DESCRIBED AS A DEPRAVED KILLER DRIVEN BY LUST AND
COCAINE AS HIS TRIAL ON SIX MURDER CHARGES GOT UNDER
WAY.
BUT SULLY'S ATTORNEY—DOUGLAS GRAY—SAID IN YESTER-
DAY'S (TUESDAY'S) OPENING STATEMENT THAT THE EVIDENCE
LINKING THE 41-YEAR-OLD DEFENDANT TO THE SIX 1983 KILLINGS
IS NOT ENOUGH TO PROVE HIS GUILT BEYOND A REASONABLE
DOUBT.
GRAY ALSO SAID SULLY WAS MERELY A BUSINESSMAN WHO
BECAME OBSESSED WITH COCAINE AND FEMALE COMPANION-
SHIP. BUT ASSISTANT DISTRICT ATTORNEY TOM STEVENS SAID
THOSE DESIRES DROVE SULLY TO COMMIT THE CRIMES.
        AP-LA-04-09-86 1007 T
168
UF
AP-BUSINESSWATCH
DOW JONES 1:00 STOCK AVERAGES

30 INDUSTRIAL	1780.77	UP	11.01
20 TRANSPORTATIONS	791.46	UP	3.06
15 UTILITIES	188.55	UP	0.92
65 STOCKS	697.57	UP	3.76

TRADING: HEAVY

    AP-LA-04-09-86 1008 T

B169

  UB

AP-URGENT-U-S-TERRORISM(TOPS)

(WASHINGTON)—THE DEFENSE DEPARTMENT HAS GIVEN ITS CLEAREST SIGNAL YET THAT PLANS ARE BEING CONSIDERED FOR A MILITARY STRIKE AGAINST LIBYA.

SOURCES SAY THE PENTAGON HAS CANCELED THE DEPARTURE OF ONE OF ITS AIRCRAFT CARRIERS FROM THE MEDITERRANEAN.

AND THE SOURCES SAY THE NAVY HAS ALSO BEEN TOLD TO DROP PLANS FOR A LIBERTY CALL FOR THE SECOND CARRIER IN THE REGION.

THE OFFICIALS SAY THE NAVY HASN'T YET RECEIVED ORDERS TO RE-FORM A NAVAL BATTLE GROUP OFF LIBYA'S COAST.

BUT ONE SOURCE SAID IT'S BECOME CLEAR THAT—AS HE PUT IT—"WE'RE GOING TO HAVE TO KEEP OUR OPTIONS OPEN FOR THE MOMENT BY KEEPING TWO CARRIERS OVER THERE."

PRESIDENT REAGAN TODAY TOLD NEWSPAPER EDITORS IN WASHINGTON THAT THE U-S IS "NOT GOING TO JUST SIT HERE AND HOLD STILL" IN THE WAKE OF RENEWED TERRORIST AT-TACKS AGAINST AMERICANS IN EUROPE.

    AP-LA-04-09-86 1010 T

B170

  UN

AP-(VOYAGER-NEPTUNE)

(PASADENA, CALIF. (AP)—NASA SAYS THE ROUTE OF THE VOY-AGER SPACECRAFT TO ITS 1989 ENCOUNTER WITH NEPTUNE WILL BE CHANGED IF NECESSARY TO PREVENT THE PROBE FROM BEING DESTROYED BY BOULDERS OR PEBBLES ORBITING THE PLANET.

THE CHIEF SPOKESMAN AT NASA'S JET PROPULSION LABORA-TORY IN PASADENA, FRANK BRISTOW, SAID NASA WILL NOT JEOP-ARDIZE THE AIRCRAFT.

BRISTOW SAID SCIENTISTS WILL SPEND THE NEXT COUPLE OF YEARS TRYING TO DETERMINE THE PRECISE LOCATION AND EX-TENT OF PARTIAL RINGS OF BOULDERS, PEBBLES OR DUST ENCIR-CLING NEPTUNE.

THEY WILL TRY TO DETERMINE WHETHER VOYAGER'S PLANNED ROUTE POSES A HIGH RISK OF COLLISIONS BETWEEN THE SPACE PROBE AND ROCKS IN THE RINGS.

HOWEVER, DEPUTY VOYAGER PROJECT SCIENTIST ELLIS MINER

SAID YESTERDAY RESEARCHERS PREFER TO STICK WITH VOYAG-
ER'S PLANNED TRAJECTORY BECAUSE IT WILL TAKE THE PROBE
AND ITS CAMERAS CLOSE TO NEPTUNE'S MOON TRITON.

THE MOON APPARENTLY HAS ORGANIC SLUDGE, METHANE ICE
AND POSSIBLY LAKES OF LIQUID NITROGEN ON ITS SURFACE.

(JSF)

AP-LA-04-09-86 1013 T

B171

UF

AP-BUSINESSWATCH

N-Y-S-E TRANSACTIONS

	TODAY	PREVIOUS SESSION
12-1	19,750,000	22,980,000
9:30-1	98,680,000	104,920,000

AP-LA-04-09-86 1014 T

B172

UO

AP-(NORCAL ZONE FORECASTS)

NORTHWEST CALIFORNIA—COASTAL LOW CLOUDS AND FOG
WITH PARTIAL AFTERNOON CLEARING TODAY. INLAND . . . A FEW
CLOUDS NORTH OTHERWISE SUNNY. HIGHS IN THE UPPER 50S TO
MID 70S. NORTHERLY WINDS TO 20 MPH NEAR THE OCEAN WITH
LIGHTER WINDS INLAND . . TONIGHT . . . COASTAL LOW CLOUDS
AND FOG WITH LOCAL DRIZZLE . . . MAINLY NORTH OF SHELTER
COVE. PARTLY CLOUDY NORTH INLAND AND FAIR SOUTH. LOWS
IN THE 40S TO LOW 50S. NORTHERLY WINDS TO 20 MPH NEAR THE
OCEAN WITH LIGHTER WINDS INLAND . . TOMORROW . . . MOSTLY
CLOUDY NORTH OF SHELTER COVE AND ALONG THE COAST. LO-
CAL DRIZZLE. SUNNY SOUTH WITH PATCHY MORNING FOG OR
LOW CLOUDS. HIGHS IN THE MID 50S TO LOW 70S.

SAN FRANCISCO BAY REGION—PATCHY MORNING LOW CLOUDS
OR FOG TODAY BECOMING MOSTLY SUNNY. HIGHS IN THE 60S TO
MID 70S. WESTERLY WINDS INCREASING TO 20 MPH NORTH BAY
. . . OTHERWISE LIGHT WINDS . . TONIGHT . . . FAIR EXCEPT IN-
CREASING LOW CLOUDS OR FOG . . SPREADING INLAND OVER-
NIGHT. LOWS IN THE 40S TO LOW 50S. WESTERLY EVENING WINDS
TO 20 MPH DECREASING DURING THE NIGHT . . TOMORROW . . .
MORNING LOW CLOUDS OR FOG . . . BECOMING MOSTLY SUNNY
WITH HIGHS IN THE 60S TO MID 70S.

CENTRAL COAST FROM MONTEREY TO POINT CONCEPTION—
MOSTLY SUNNY. HIGHS IN THE MID 60S TO MID 70S. NORTHWEST
WINDS INCREASING TO 20 MPH THIS AFTERNOON . . TONIGHT
. . . . FAIR EXCEPT FOR PATCHY LATE NIGHT FOG. LOWS IN THE
UPPER 30S AND 40S. WESTERLY EVENING WINDS TO 20 MPH DIMIN-
ISHING DURING THE NIGHT . . TOMORROW . . . SUNNY EXCEPT

FOR PATCHY MORNING FOG. HIGHS IN THE 60S TO MID 70S.

SALINAS VALLEY AND ENVIRONS—MOSTLY SUNNY. HIGHS IN THE MID 60S TO MID 70S. NORTHWEST AFTERNOON WINDS TO 15 MPH . . TONIGHT . . . FAIR EXCEPT FOR PATCHY LATE NIGHT FOG. LOW IN THE UPPER 30S AND 40S. LIGHT NORTHWEST WINDS . . TO-MORROW . . . SUNNY EXCEPT FOR PATCHY EARLY MORNING FOG. HIGHS 65 TO 75.

SAN JOAQUIN VALLEY—SUNNY EXCEPT FOR PATCHY MORNING LOW CLOUDS OR FOG. HIGHS IN THE UPPER 60S AND 70S. NORTH-WEST WINDS TO 15 MPH . . TONIGHT . . . FAIR WITH LOWS IN THE 40S TO LOW 50S. LIGHT NORTH WINDS . . TOMORROW . . . SUNNY WITH HIGHS IN THE UPPER 60S AND 70S.

SACRAMENTO VALLEY—MOSTLY SUNNY AFTER PATCHY MORN-ING FOG SOUTH OF CHICO. HIGH IN THE UPPER 60S TO MID 70S. LIGHT NORTH WINDS . . TONIGHT . . . FAIR WITH LOWS IN THE 40S TO LOW 50S. NORTHERLY WINDS TO 15 MPH NORTH END OF VAL-LEY WITH LIGHTER WINDS ELSEWHERE . . TOMORROW . . . MOSTLY SUNNY WITH HIGHS IN THE UPPER 60S AND 70S.

MOUNT SHASTA-SISKIYOU AREA—VARIABLE CLOUDS WITH HIGHS IN THE MID 50S TO MID 60S. NORTHWEST WINDS TO 20 MPH . . TONIGHT . . . PARTLY CLOUDY WITH LOWS IN THE 30S TO THE LOWER 40S. NORTHERLY WINDS TO 15 MPH . . TOMORROW . . . PARTLY CLOUDY WITH HIGHS IN THE 50S TO THE LOW 60S.

NORTHEAST CALIFORNIA—VARIABLE CLOUDS WITH HIGHS IN THE 50S. NORTHWEST WINDS TO 15 MPH . . TONIGHT . . . PARTLY CLOUDY. LOWS IN THE UPPER 20S AND 30S. LIGHT NORTHWEST WINDS . . TOMORROW . . . PARTLY CLOUDY WITH HIGHS IN THE 50S.

NORTHERN SIERRA NEVADA—MOSTLY SUNNY . . TONIGHT . . . FAIR . . TOMORROW . . . MOSTLY SUNNY.

SOUTHERN SIERRA NEVADA—MOSTLY SUNNY . . TONIGHT AND TOMORROW . . . FAIR.

  AP-LA-04-09-86 1023 T

B173

  UR

AP-NETWORK 1:32 PES, 4-9-86 (TWO TAKES)

[*What follows is the transmission schedule for AP's audio service.*]

KHADAFY THREATS

147-V-39-TRIPOLI, LIBYA-(KEVIN COSTELLOE)-AT FIRST NEWS CONF. SINCE U-S-LIBYAN HOSTILITIES, MOAMMAR KHADAFY CLAIMS PLANS HAVE BEEN COMPLETED FOR ATTACK AGAINST U-S. (NEEDS HD LEAD)

148-A-13-TRIPOLI, LIBYA-(COL. MOAMMAR KHADAFY, SPKG.

THROUGH INTERPRETER, AT NEWS CONF.)-"THE WORLD"-U-S WILL BE DEFEATED IN ANY MILITARY ACTION.

149-A-20-(A-P CORR. KEVIN COSTELLOE)-"ARAB WORLD"- LIBYAN LDR. MOAMMAR KHADAFY SAYS PLANS MADE FOR MILI- TARY CONFRONTATION W- U-S.

150-A-25-(KEVIN COSTELLOE)-"HE'S SAYING"-LIBYAN LDR.'S REMARKS CONTAIN DISCREPANCIES.

REAGAN-TERRORISM

151-W-38-WASH-(CANDY CROWLEY W- PRES. REAGAN)-PRES. SAYS U-S WON'T TAKE TERRORIST ATTACKS LYING DOWN.

152-A-12-(PRES. REAGAN, ADDR. MTG. OF AMER. ASSN. OF NEWSPAPER EDS)-"INTELLIGENCE MATTERS"-U-S WILL ACT AGAINST TERRORISM.

LIBYA-U-S

153-V-37-WASH-(KAREN SLOAN)-NEW SIGNS OF POSSIBLE U-S MILITARY ACTION AGAINST LIBYA.

154-A-15-(A-P CORR. KAREN SLOAN)-"OPTIONS OPEN"-NEW OR- DERS WILL KEEP TWO U-S AIRCRAFT CARRIERS AT SEA IN THE MEDITERRANEAN.

LIBYA-W. GERMANY

155-V-27-BONN-(KEN JAUTZ)-W. GERMANY DENIES CAVING IN TO PRESSURE FROM U-S TO TAKE ACTION AGAINST LIBYA.

156-V-34-STATE DEPT-(BARRY SCHWEID)-U-S CITES LIBYAN LINK TO NIGHTCLUB BOMBING IN EXPULSION OF LIBYAN DIPLOMATS FROM WEST GERMANY.

AP-LA-04-09-86 1027 T

B174

UB

AP-URGENT-SPACE SHUTTLE(TOPS)

(CAPE CANAVERAL, FLORIDA)—WHEN THE DEBRIS OF THE SHUTTLE "CHALLENGER" HIT THE ATLANTIC OCEAN ON JANU- ARY 28TH—THE CREW CABIN ITSELF WAS IN ONE PIECE.

THAT REPORT COMES TODAY FROM A FEDERAL SAFETY INVES- TIGATOR.

TERRY ARMENTROUT—WHO HEADS THE NATIONAL TRANSPOR- TATION SAFETY BOARD'S BUREAU OF ACCIDENT INVESTIGA- TION—SAYS THE CREW CABIN WAS INSIDE THE NOSE SECTION OF THE SPACE SHUTTLE AFTER THE EXPLOSION—AND THAT'S HOW IT HIT THE OCEAN.

ARMENTROUT SAYS WHEN THE NOSE SECTION HIT THE WATER—IT HAD THE CREW MODULE INSIDE IT.

BUT MOST EXPERTS DON'T THINK THE ASTRONAUTS SURVIVED THE NINE-MILE PLUNGE TO THE OCEAN. THEY BELIEVE INSTEAD THAT THE SEVEN WERE PROBABLY KILLED INSTANTLY FROM THE

SHOCK OF THE EXPLOSION. AND IF NOT, IT'S BELIEVED THE CREW
WAS KILLED FROM AERODYNAMIC FORCES AS THE NOSE SECTION
AND THE CABIN INSIDE IT TUMBLED FROM THE SKY.

ARMENTROUT SAYS THE SHUTTLE BROKE APART MORE FROM
AERODYNAMIC FORCES AND WATER IMPACT THAN FROM THE
FORCE OF THE EXPLOSION.

IN FACT, HE SAYS, THERE WAS NO LARGE EXPLOSION. ACCORD-
ING TO ARMENTROUT, THE CLOUD OF SMOKE AND FLAME THAT
WAS SEEN AT THE TIME OF THE ACCIDENT RESULTED PRIMARILY
FROM THE BREAKUP OF THE LARGE EXTERNAL FUEL TANK—AND
FROM THE FIRES THAT RESULTED WHEN THE OXYGEN AND HY-
DROGEN FROM THE TANK MIXED AND BURNED.

     AP-LA-04-09-86 1031 T

B175

   UR

AP-NETWORK 1:32 PES, 4-9-86 TAKE-2

[*The second part of AP's audio feed*]

   BUSH-KHADAFY

157-V-31-W-THE V-P IN OMAN-(TERRY HUNT)-V-P HITS HARD AT
LIBYAN LDR. KHADAFY.

158-A-17-ABOARD U-S-S ENTERPRISE-(V-P GEO. BUSH, ADDRESS-
ING CREW, IN GULF OF OMAN)-''THE MEDITERRANEAN''-NAVY
PILOTS DID COMMENDABLE JOB RETALIATING AGAINST LIBYAN
FORCES.

159-A-17-(V-P GEO. BUSH)-''THREE FEET''(CHEERS FADE)-CON-
TRARY TO SOME OPINIONS, U-S PILOTS WHO ATTACKED LIBYAN
POSITIONS DID NOT IMPROVE LIBYAN LEADER'S IMAGE.

   SHUTTLE

160-V-35-KENNEDY SPACE CENTER-(MARK KNOLLER)-NASA OFFI-
CIAL SAYS 'CHALLENGER'S' CREW COMPARTMENT WAS INTACT
AS IT HIT WATER. (NEEDS HD LEAD)

161-A-20-(A-P CORR. MARK KNOLLER, DURING TOUR OF HANGER
WHERE SHUTTLE DEBRIS BEING KEPT)-''THE DISASTER''-LARGE
NASA BUILDING FILLED WITH PIECES OF SHUTTLE.

162-A-23-(MARK KNOLLER, DURING TOUR)-''BEEN RECOVERED''
PERHAPS ONLY A FIFTH OF THE SPACE SHUTTLE HAS BEEN RE-
COVERED AND IDENTIFIED.

     AP-LA-04-09-86 1033 T

B176

   UN

AP-(DEADLY CHEESE)

(BELLFLOWER)—JALISCO MEXICAN PRODUCTS AND ITS PRESI-
DENT PLEADED INNOCENT TODAY TO 60 CHARGES STEMMING

FROM AN EPIDEMIC IN WHICH THE COMPANY'S CHEESE WAS
BLAMED FOR AT LEAST 39 DEATHS.

GARY MCPHERSON AND HIS COMPANY ENTERED THEIR PLEAS
BEFORE JUDGE JAMES PEARCE IN LOS CERRITOS MUNICIPAL
COURT, PART OF THE LOS ANGELES COUNTY COURT SYSTEM.
PEARCE SCHEDULED A PRETRIAL HEARING APRIL 17.

A CRIMINAL COMPLAINT ACCUSES JALISCO AND MCPHERSON
OF 60 MISDEMEANOR VIOLATIONS OF CALIFORNIA AGRICUL-
TURAL, HEALTH AND SAFETY CODES, INCLUDING SALE OF ADUL-
TERATED FOOD.

JALISCO'S VICE PRESIDENT, JOSE LUIS MEDINA, HAS PLEADED
NO CONTEST TO 12 OF THE 60 COUNTS AND FACES SENTENCING
MAY 20TH.

THE CHARGES STEM FROM LAST SUMMER'S OUTBREAK OF THE
BACTERIAL DISEASE LISTERIOSIS. THE EPIDEMIC PROMPTED PER-
MANENT CLOSURE OF JALISCO'S CHEESE FACTORY IN ARTESIA
AND A NATIONWIDE RECALL OF ITS SOFT, MEXICAN-STYLE
CHEESES.

(JSF)

AP-LA-04-09-86 1036 T

B177

UN

AP-MIDWIFE

(SONORA)—TUOLUMNE COUNTY SUPERVISORS GAVE PERMIS-
SION TO HIRE A MIDWIFE FOR PREGNANT WOMEN ON MEDI-CAL
BECAUSE DOCTORS ARE REFUSING TO ACCEPT NEW PATIENTS UN-
DER THE PROGRAM.

ABOUT 120 WOMEN A YEAR WOULD BE SERVED BY THE NURSE-
MIDWIFE AUTHORIZED YESTERDAY ON A UNANIMOUS VOTE. THE
MIDWIFE WILL SEE WOMEN AT TUOLUMNE GENERAL HOSPITAL
AND ATTEND DELIVERIES AT SIERRA HOSPITAL.

THE LAST OF THREE SONORA DOCTORS TAKING MEDI-CAL PA-
TIENTS WITHDREW FROM THE PROGRAM IN JANUARY, MAINLY
BECAUSE OF FALLING REIMBURSEMENT AND DELAYS IN PAY-
MENTS.

AP-GOLD MINE

(SONORA)—A PERMIT HAS BEEN APPROVED FOR A 40 (M) MIL-
LION DOLLAR GOLD-MINING PROJECT IN TUOLUMNE COUNTY,
BUT THE MINING COMPANY SAYS IT MAY HAVE TO SPEND UP TO
NINE (M) MILLION DOLLARS TO MEET SPECIAL CONDITIONS.

THE COUNTY PLANNING COMMISSION TACKED 45 CONDITIONS
ONTO THE PERMIT APPROVED YESTERDAY FOR SONORA MINING
CORPORATION FOR THE PROJECT WEST OF JAMESTOWN.

AP-LA-04-09-86 1039 T

B178
UN
AP-(ANTISPY)
(SAN DIEGO)—TIGHTER ANTI-ESPIONAGE CONTROLS AND DIS-
CUSSIONS DESIGNED TO APPEAL TO AN INDIVIDUAL'S PATRIO-
TISM ARE PART OF A NAVY PLAN TO BETTER PROTECT THE NA-
TION'S DEFENSE SECRETS.

THE COMMANDER-IN-CHIEF OF THE PACIFIC FLEET, NAVY ADMI-
RAL JAMES LYONS, SAID THE NAVY WANTS TO GET TO THE CORE
OF THE PROBLEM CREATED BY A SMALL GROUP OF SAILORS WHO
SOLD SECRETS ABROAD WITHOUT REGARD TO THE CONSE-
QUENCES.

THE ANTI-ESPIONAGE EDUCATION PROGRAM IS INTENDED TO
APPEAL TO SAILORS' INDIVIDUAL SENSE OF LOYALTY, PATRIO-
TISM AND MORAL INTEGRITY. THE PROGRAM WILL INCLUDE REG-
ULAR INSPECTIONS OF SECURITY PROCEDURES AT EACH PACIFIC
FLEET COMMAND.

LYONS' ANNOUNCEMENT COINCIDES WITH THE SAN FRANCISCO
ESPIONAGE TRIAL OF FORMER SAILOR JERRY WITWORTH, WHO IS
FACING CHARGES OF ESPIONAGE IN CONNECTION WITH THE
WALKER FAMILY SPY RING. WHITWORTH AND CONVICTED SPY
JOHN WALKER WERE NAVY RADIOMEN.

(JSF)
    AP-LA-04-09-86 1041 T
B179
    UF
AP-BUSINESSWATCH
DOW JONES 1:30 STOCK AVERAGES

30 INDUSTRIALS	1779.81	UP	10.05
20 TRANSPORTATIONS	791.46	UP	3.06
15 UTILITIES	188.81	UP	1.18
65 STOCKS	697.49	UP	3.68

    AP- LA-04-09-86 1042 T
B180
    UA
AP-NUCLEAR TEST
(LAS VEGAS, NEVADA)—THERE HAD BEEN WORD THAT THE
FEDERAL GOVERNMENT WOULD TRY AGAIN TODAY TO CONDUCT
THE NUCLEAR WEAPONS TEST THAT WAS POSTPONED YESTER-
DAY.

BUT SO FAR, THERE'S BEEN NO INDICATION THAT THE TEST HAS
TAKEN PLACE.

THE U-S DEPARTMENT OF ENERGY HASN'T CONFIRMED THAT
THE TEST WAS RE-SCHEDULED FOR TODAY—OR THAT IT WAS
ORIGINALLY SET FOR YESTERDAY.

BUT SENATOR EDWARD KENNEDY OF MASSACHUSETTS SAID HE HAD BEEN TOLD THAT THE TEST HAD BEEN RE-SCHEDULED FOR TODAY AT THE NEVADA DESERT TEST SITE.

AP-LA-04-09-86 1044 T

B181

RO

AP-FOREIGN TEMPERATURES

	HIGH	LOW	
AMSTERDAM	46	39	CLOUDY
ATHENS	81	57	CLEAR
BANGKOK	93	81	CLEAR
BARBADOS	86	73	CLEAR
BELGRADE	79	63	CLEAR
BERLIN	41	39	RAIN
BERMUDA	73	66	CLOUDY
BOGOTA	64	50	RAIN
BRUSSELS	50	32	CLOUDY
BUENOS AIRES	77	66	CLOUDY
CAIRO	77	57	CLEAR
CALGARY	77	34	CLEAR
COPENHAGEN	48	32	CLEAR
DUBLIN	45	37	CLEAR
FRANKFURT	59	45	CLOUDY
GENEVA	59	39	CLEAR
HAVANA	88	63	CLEAR
HELSINKI	43	30	CLEAR
HONG KONG	77	72	CLOUDY
ISTANBUL	64	46	CLOUDY
JO'BURG	81	54	CLEAR
KIEV	73	55	CLOUDY
LIMA	75	64	CLEAR
LISBON	52	39	RAIN
LONDON	50	37	CLEAR
MADRID	50	32	CLEAR
MANILA	93	75	CLEAR
MEXICO CITY	82	54	CLEAR
MONTREAL	48	41	RAIN
MOSCOW	41	32	CLOUDY
NASSAU	82	55	CLEAR
NEW DELHI	97	67	CLEAR
NICOSIA	78	63	CLEAR
OLSO	50	28	CLOUDY
PARIS	48	41	CLOUDY
PEKING	68	46	CLOUDY
RIO	89	68	CLEAR

	HIGH	LOW	
ROME	73	50	CLOUDY
SAN JUAN	82	71	RAIN
SANTIAGO	82	45	CLEAR
SAO PAULO	77	68	CLOUDY
SEOUL	72	50	CLOUDY
SINGAPORE	88	77	CLEAR
SYDNEY	75	64	CLOUDY
TAIPEI	84	70	CLEAR
TOKYO	72	50	CLEAR
TORONTO	46	41	CLOUDY
VANCOUVER	61	46	CLOUDY
VIENNA	75	52	CLEAR
WARSAW	73	43	CLEAR

AP-LA-04-09-86 1048 T

B182

UQ

AP-SPORTSWATCH

HERE IS THE LATEST FROM THE BALLPARKS:

AMERICAN LEAGUE

BOSTON AT DETROIT—JUST UNDER WAY

STARTERS: FRANK TANANA, DETROIT

OIL CAN BOYD, BOSTON

AP-LA-04-09-86 1049 T

B183

RH

AP-13TH NEWSMINUTE

[A 60 second "headline report" produced by AP for radio stations which sched ule quick news summaries.]

HERE IS THE LATEST NEWS FROM THE ASSOCIATED PRESS:

A FEDERAL SAFETY INSPECTOR SAYS THE CREW CABIN OF "CHALLENGER" WAS IN ONE PIECE WHEN IT HIT THE ATLANTIC AFTER THE SHUTTLE EXPLOSION IN JANUARY. THE INSPECTOR SAYS THE CABIN WAS INSIDE THE NOSE SECTION OF THE SHUT-TLE. BUT EXPERTS DON'T BELIEVE THE CREW SURVIVED THE NINE-MILE PLUNGE TO THE OCEAN—IF THEY SURVIVED THE BLAST ITSELF.

LIBYAN LEADER MOAMMAR KHADAFY SAYS PLANS ARE COM-PLETE FOR ATTACKS AGAINST AMERICAN MILITARY AND CIVIL-IAN TARGETS AROUND THE WORLD. KHADAFY HELD A NEWS CONFERENCE IN HIS HEAVILY-GUARDED BUNKER IN TRIPOLI.

SPEAKING TO A GROUP OF NEWSPAPER EDITORS IN WASHING-TON TODAY, PRESIDENT REAGAN DECLARED THAT KHADAFY IS

"DEFINITELY A SUSPECT" IN THE FATAL BOMBINGS ABOARD A T-W-A JETLINER OVER GREECE AND THE BERLIN NIGHTCLUB. AND REAGAN WARNED THAT THE U-S WILL RESPOND.

THERE ARE SIGNS TODAY THAT LAST MONTH'S MEXICANA AIR-LINES CRASH WAS NO ACCIDENT. THE HEAD OF AN INTERNA-TIONAL PILOTS GROUP SAYS IT LOOKS LIKE IT WAS SABOTAGE. TWO GROUPS HAVE CLAIMED THEY DOWNED THE PLANE IN RE-TALIATION FOR U-S MILITARY STRIKES AGAINST LIBYA. THE CRASH KILLED ALL 166 PEOPLE ON BOARD, INCLUDING NINE AMERICANS.

      AP-LA-04-09-86 1052 T

B184

  UG

  AP-(CALIFORNIA UPDATE)

[*Each of the wire services delivers news stories specifically tailored to state and regional interests*]

(BELLFLOWER)—INNOCENT PLEAS WERE ENTERED TODAY BY JALISCO MEXICAN PRODUCTS AND ITS PRESIDENT TO CHARGES STEMMING FROM LAST SUMMER'S EPIDEMIC IN WHICH THE COM-PANY'S CHEESE WAS BLAMED FOR AT LEAST 39 DEATHS. THE COMPANY AND PRESIDENT GARY MCPHERSON ARE CHARGED WITH 60 MISDEMEANOR VIOLATIONS OF CALIFORNIA AGRICUL-TURAL, HEALTH AND SAFETY CODES, INCLUDING SALE OF ADUL-TERATED FOOD.

(SAN DIEGO)—THE NAVY IS TAKING STEPS TO BETTER PROTECT THE NATION'S DEFENSE SECRETS. THROUGH DISCUSSION, THE NAVY'S PACIFIC DIVISION PLANS TO APPEAL TO SAILORS' INDI-VIDUAL SENSE OF LOYALTY, PATRIOTISM AND MORAL INTEGRITY IN THE HOPE THAT IT WILL CURB THE SPY PROBLEM.

(SAN MATEO)—FORMER POLICEMAN ANTHONY "JACK" SULLY WAS DESCRIBED AS A DEPRAVED KILLER DRIVEN BY LUST AND COCAINE AS HIS TRIAL ON SIX MURDER CHARGES GOT UNDER WAY IN SAN MATEO. BUT SULLY'S ATTORNEY CLAIMS THE EVI-DENCE LINKING THE 41-YEAR-OLD DEFENDANT TO THE 1983 KILL-INGS IS NOT ENOUGH TO PROVE HIS GUILT BEYOND A REASON-ABLE DOUBT.

(SONORA)—TUOLUMNE COUNTY SUPERVISORS GAVE PERMIS-SION TO HIRE A MIDWIFE FOR PREGNANT WOMEN ON MEDI-CAL BECAUSE DOCTORS ARE REFUSING TO ACCEPT NEW PATIENTS UN-DER THE PROGRAM. ABOUT 120 WOMEN A YEAR WOULD BE SERVED BY THE NURSE-MIDWIFE.

(VANCOUVER, BRITISH COLUMBIA)—THE VANCOUVER CITY COUNCIL HAS VOTED UNANIMOUSLY TO SET UP A SISTER-CITY

ARRANGEMENT WITH LOS ANGELES. THE ARRANGEMENT STILL
MUST BE APPROVED BY THE LOS ANGELES COUNCIL.
  (JSF)
        AP-LA-04-09-86 1056 T
B185
  RR
  AP-NETWORK ADVISORY
[*The wire services often include information about up-coming material including
audio programming available to those subscribing to the service.*]

FORMER BUDGET DIRECTOR DAVID STOCKMAN WILL GIVE HIS
FIRST BROADCAST INTERVIEW ABOUT HIS CONTROVERSIAL NEW
BOOK IN THIS WEEK'S EDITION OF "NEWSWEEK ON AIR".
  STOCKMAN'S "THE TRIUMPH OF POLITICS: WHY THE REAGAN
REVOLUTION FAILED" MAKES SOME TOUGH JUDGMENTS ABOUT
THE PEOPLE STOCKMAN WORKED WITH IN WASHINGTON, IN-
CLUDING THE PRESIDENT.
  STOCKMAN WILL BE INTERVIEWED BY NEWSWEEK SENIOR EDI-
TOR DAVID ALPERN AND AP NETWORK NEWS CORRESPONDENT
MARK KNOLLER.
  NEWSWEEK ON AIR IS A PRODUCTION OF AP NETWORK NEWS
AND NEWSWEEK MAGAZINE. IT RUNS AT 7:06AES SUNDAY MORN-
ING, AND IS REPEATED AT 10:06AES.
  AP NETWORK NEWS-WASHINGTON
        AP-LA-04-09-86 1058
B186
  RA
  AP-LAROUCHE
  (WASHINGTON)—IN WHAT'S BELIEVED TO BE HIS FIRST PUBLIC
APPEARANCE SINCE TWO OF HIS SUPPORTERS WON IN LAST
MONTH'S ILLINOIS PRIMARY—POLITICAL EXTREMIST LYNDON
LAROUCHE TODAY SAID THE SOVIET GOVERNMENT AND INTER-
NATIONAL DRUG DEALERS ARE TRYING TO KILL HIM.
  AT A NEWS CONFERENCE IN WASHINGTON, LAROUCHE ALSO
SAID PRESIDENT REAGAN'S CHIEF OF STAFF, DONALD REGAN,
SHOULD BE IN JAIL. LAROUCHE CHARGED THAT REGAN WAS TIED
TO DRUG MONEY "LAUNDERING" EFFORTS OF WALL STREET
FIRMS.
  DURING THE NATIONAL PRESS CLUB NEWS CONFERENCE,
LAROUCHE REPEATEDLY ACCUSED THE SOVIET GOVERNMENT,
THE BRITISH GOVERNMENT, DRUG DEALERS, INTERNATIONAL
BANKERS AND SOME JOURNALISTS OF BEING INVOLVED IN
WORLD-WIDE CONSPIRACIES.
        AP-LA-04-09-86 1101 T

B187

RH

AP-14TH NEWSMINUTE

HERE IS THE LATEST NEWS FROM THE ASSOCIATED PRESS:

SOURCES SAY THE PENTAGON HAS CANCELED AN AIRCRAFT CARRIER'S ORDERS TO RETURN HOME FROM THE MEDITERRANEAN SEA. ALSO, THE SOURCES SAY THE NAVY IS CANCELLING SHORE LEAVE FOR SAILORS ABOARD A SECOND CARRIER. THESE ACTIONS FOLLOW WORD FROM A U-S OFFICIAL THAT PLANS ARE BEING STUDIED FOR A MILITARY STRIKE AGAINST LIBYA.

SPEAKING TO NEWSPAPER EDITORS GATHERED IN WASHINGTON, PRESIDENT REAGAN SAID THE U-S IS "NOT GOING TO JUST SIT HERE AND HOLD STILL" IN THE WAKE OF RENEWED TERRORIST ATTACKS AGAINST AMERICANS IN EUROPE. REAGAN CALLED KHADAFY A DEFINITE SUSPECT IN THE RECENT T-W-A AIRPLANE AND WEST BERLIN NIGHTCLUB BOMBINGS.

LIBYAN LEADER KHADAFY (KAH-DAH'-FEE) SEEMS TO BE ANTICIPATING TROUBLE. HE SUMMONED REPORTERS TO HIS SANDBAGGED BUNKER TODAY TO SAY HIS MILITARY PLANS ARE COMPLETE TO CHALLENGE THE U-S. KHADAFY RENEWED THREATS AGAINST AMERICAN MILITARY AND CIVILIAN TARGETS.

THE HEAD OF AN INTERNATIONAL PILOTS GROUP SAYS THERE'S EVIDENCE THAT A BOMB CAUSED LAST WEEK'S CRASH OF A MEXICANA AIRLINES JET. ALL 166 PEOPLE ABOARD WERE KILLED. REG SMITH OF THE PILOTS GROUP SAYS HE BELIEVE'S THERE WAS AN EXPLOSION ABOARD, PROBABLY FROM A BOMB.

A FEDERAL SAFETY INSPECTOR SAYS THE SPACE SHUTTLE "CHALLENGER'S" CREW CABIN HIT THE SURFACE OF THE ATLANTIC OCEAN INTACT AFTER THE JANUARY 28TH EXPLOSION. HOWEVER, MOST EXPERTS BELIEVE THE SEVEN ASTRONAUTS WERE KILLED INSTANTLY FROM THE SHOCK OF THE BLAST.

AP-LA-04-09-86 1105 T

B188

RS

AP-AFTERNOON SPORTSWATCH (TWO TAKES)

[*This means the story will be interrupted for other stories; a warning to look for more material.*]

FOR THE 16 N-H-L TEAMS SURVIVING THE 80-GAME REGULAR SEASON, TONIGHT BEGINS THE "SECOND SEASON"—MORE FORMALLY KNOWN AS THE STANLEY CUP PLAYOFFS. EIGHT BEST-OF-FIVE SHOWDOWNS FACE OFF ACROSS NORTH AMERICA.

THE EDMONTON OILERS ENTER THE PLAYOFF CHASE HEAVILY FAVORED TO MAKE IT THREE STRAIGHT STANLEY CUPS. EDMON-

TON'S QUEST BEGINS AGAINST THE VANCOUVER CANUCKS—A
CLUB THAT TOTALED 59 POINTS IN THE STANDINGS—60 LESS
THAN THE POWERFUL OILERS. STILL, POSTING THE TOP REGULAR-
SEASON RECORD HAD ITS DISADVANTAGES. ACCORDING TO ED-
MONTON COACH GLEN SATHER, "EVERYWHERE WE GO, THEY'RE
GUNNING FOR US. BELIEVE ME IT WEARS ON YOU."

ELSEWHERE ON N-H-L PLAYOFF ICE THIS EVENING, THE WINNI-
PEG JETS BEGIN PLAY IN CALGARY AGAINST THE FLAMES. IN MIN-
NESOTA, THE NORTH STARS HOST THE ST. LOUIS BLUES. THE TO-
RONTO MAPLE LEAFS OPEN AGAINST THE BLACKHAWKS AT
CHICAGO STADIUM.

THE MONTREAL CANADIENS ENTERTAIN THE BOSTON BRUINS.
THE HARTFORD WHALERS MAKE THEIR FIRST POST-SEASON AP-
PEARANCE IN SIX YEARS WHEN THEY TRAVEL TO PLAY THE NOR-
DIQUES IN QUEBEC CITY. IN PHILADELPHIA, THE FLYERS—WITH
THE SECOND-BEST REGULAR-SEASON RECORD—TAKE ON THE
NEW YORK RANGERS. AND NEW YORK'S ISLANDERS TRY TO EX-
TEND THEIR STANLEY CUP HEX OVER THE HOMETOWN WASHING-
TON CAPITALS. THE ISLES HAVE KNOCKED THE CAPS OUT OF THE
PLAYOFFS THE PAST THREE YEARS.

     AP-LA-04-09-86 1109 T

B189

   UN

  AP-(UNOCAL RETIREMENT)

  (LOS ANGELES)—A CONTINUING DROP IN OIL PRICES HAS
PROMPTED UNOCAL TO TRY TO PARE ITS WORK FORCE WITH AN
EARLY RETIREMENT OFFER THE COMPANY SAID IS EXPECTED TO
ATTRACT ABOUT ONE-THOUSAND EMPLOYEES.

IN A LETTER TO WORKERS, COMPANY OFFICIALS SAID COST-
CUTTING IS NECESSARY BECAUSE THE INDUSTRY IS UNDER SE-
VERE ATTACK DUE TO THE PREDATORY PRICING OF THE OIL EX-
PORTING NATIONS.

DESPITE THE OIL INDUSTRY'S RETRENCHMENT AFTER OIL
PRICES BEGAN TO DECLINE IN 1981, UNOCAL'S WORLDWIDE EM-
PLOYMENT HAS REMAINED AT ABOUT 20-THOUSAND.

COMPANY OFFICIALS SAID THEY DON'T HAVE AN EMPLOYMENT
GOAL IN MIND, BUT THEY EXPECT ABOUT TWO-THIRDS OF THE 16-
HUNDRED WORKERS ELIGIBLE FOR THE PROGRAM TO TAKE THE
OFFER, AIMED AT NON-UNION EMPLOYEES WHO REACH AGE 55 BY
JUNE 30TH. SENIOR MANAGERS ARE EXCLUDED.

  (JSF)

     AP-LA-04-09-86 1111 T

B190

  UF

  AP-BUSINESSWATCH

WALL STREET (TOPS)

(NEW YORK)—STOCK PRICES HAVE TURNED MIXED IN HEAVY
TRADING. THE DOW JONES INDUSTRIAL AVERAGE IS OFF NEARLY
FOUR POINTS. AND ADVANCING ISSUES LEAD LOSERS BY A NAR-
ROW MARGIN.

THE MARKET HAD BEEN HIGHER.

DOW JONES 2:00 STOCK AVERAGES

30 INDUSTRIALS	1765.92	DOWN	3.84
20 TRANSPORTATIONS	786.43	DOWN	1.97
15 UTILITIES	187.47	DOWN	0.16
65 STOCKS	692.38	DOWN	1.43

AP-LA-04-09-86 1113 T

B191

RI

AP-U-N-WALDHEIM

(NEW YORK)—THE ISRAELI AMBASSADOR TO THE UNITED NA-
TIONS SAYS THE CHARGES THAT KURT WALDHEIM WAS IN-
VOLVED WITH THE NAZIS IN WORLD WAR TWO CAN NOT YET BE
PUT ASIDE.

THE AMBASSADOR MADE THE COMMENTS AFTER SPENDING
MORE THAN AN HOUR LOOKING THROUGH THE U-N WAR CRIMES
COMMISSION FILE ON WALDHEIM, THE FORMER U-N SECRETARY-
GENERAL.

ISRAELI AMBASSADOR BENJAMIN NETANYAHU DIDN'T SAY
WHAT'S IN THE U-N FILE ON WALDHEIM—WHO'S NOW A CANDI-
DATE FOR THE PRESIDENT OF AUSTRIA.

THE ISRAELI DIPLOMAT—AND AUSTRIA'S U-N AMBASSADOR—
WERE ALLOWED TO SEE THE FILE AFTER REQUESTS WERE MADE
BY THEIR GOVERNMENTS. THOSE REQUESTS FOLLOWED ALLEGA-
TIONS THAT WALDHEIM SERVED WITH A GERMAN ARMY UNIT
THAT COMMITTED ATROCITIES IN THE BALKANS DURING WORLD
WAR TWO.

THE TWO DIPLOMATS WERE ALLOWED TO COPY THE CONTENTS
OF THE FILE—AND NETANYAHU SAYS THOSE COPIES WILL BE
SENT TO ISRAEL FOR FURTHER STUDY.

WALDHEIM HAS DENIED THE ALLEGATIONS OF A NAZI PAST—
AND HAS SAID THEY'RE DESIGNED TO HURT HIS CHANCES IN THE
AUSTRIAN PRESIDENTIAL ELECTION.

AP-LA-04-09-86 1116 T

B192

UN

AP-(GATES-BALLOT)

(SANTA ANA)—ORANGE COUNTY SHERIFF BRAD GATES HAS
LOST A LEGAL ROUND TO GET ALLEGATIONS ABOUT HIM RE-
MOVED FROM A SAMPLE BALLOT.

GATES' OPPONENT, LINDA LEA CALLIGAN, SUBMITTED MATE-
RIAL FOR THE BALLOT THAT CLAIMS GATES ''HAS BEEN CON-
VICTED OF A FEDERAL CRIME AND COVERED UP A FELONY
DRUNK-DRIVING ARREST.''

THE MAILER WILL BE SENT TO ONE (M) MILLION ORANGE
COUNTY RESIDENTS.

LAST WEEK, ORANGE COUNTY SUPERIOR COURT JUDGE JUDITH
RYAN FOUND THE STATEMENTS TO BE FALSE AND MISLEADING
AND ORDERED THEM TO BE REMOVED FROM THE SAMPLE BAL-
LOT.

BY YESTERDAY, AN APPELLATE COURT RULED THEY SHOULD
REMAIN.

GATES' CAMPAIGN MANAGER CALLED THE COURT ACTION GUT-
LESS AND SAID THE STATE SUPREME COURT WOULD BE ASKED TO
THROW OUT THE ORDER.

(JSF)

AP-LA-04-09-86 1118 T

B193

UF

AP-BUSINESSWATCH

N-Y-S-E TRANSACTIONS

	TODAY	PREVIOUS SESSION
1-2	16,490,000	15,390,000
9:30-2	115,170,000	103,270,000

AP-LA-04-09-86 1119 T

B194

RS

AP-AFTERNOON SPORTSWATCH-TAKE 2

THE SAN ANTONIO SPURS CAN COMPLETE THE N-B-A PLAYOFF
ROSTER WITH A VICTORY TONIGHT. IF THE SPURS WIN IN PHOE-
NIX, THEY ELIMINATE THE SUNS AND THE LOS ANGELES CLIPPERS
FROM THE RACE FOR THE EIGHTH AND FINAL WESTERN CONFER-
ENCE SPOT. EIGHT EASTERN TEAMS HAVE ALREADY QUALIFIED.

NOW IT'S ADRIAN DANTLEY'S TURN. THE UTAH JAZZ FORWARD
PLAYS AT HOME AGAINST THE SACRAMENTO KINGS TRAILING
LEADER DOMINIQUE WILKINS OF ATLANTA BY 15-HUNDREDTHS
OF A POINT IN THE N-B-A SCORING RACE. WILKINS HAD 37 POINTS
FOR THE HAWKS LAST NIGHT AGAINST CHICAGO AND NOW OWNS
A 29-POINT-93 PER GAME AVERAGE. DENVER'S ALEX ENGLISH
TRAILS WILKINS BY NEARLY A QUARTER OF A POINT ENTERING
THE FINAL FIVE DAYS OF THE SEASON.

ENGLISH AND WILKINS HAVE THE NIGHT OFF.

THE NEW ENGLAND PATRIOTS SAY TALKS ARE STILL UNDER
WAY WITH A GROUP OF INVESTORS TO SELL THEIR HOME FIELD,
SULLIVAN STADIUM. REPORTEDLY, THE GROUP, INCLUDING FOR-

MER TRANSPORTATION SECRETARY DREW LEWIS, IS SET TO PAY
30 (M) MILLION DOLLARS FOR THE BALLPARK AND LEASES TO A
NEARBY RACE TRACK AND LAND. ACCORDING TO THE "BOSTON
HERALD," LEWIS AND HIS PARTNERS WANT TO EVENTUALLY
PURCHASE THE PATRIOTS.

IN THE MAJOR LEAGUES TONIGHT, THE NATIONAL LEAGUE
SCHEDULE FEATURES THREE GAMES—PHILADELPHIA AT CINCIN-
NATI, SAN FRANCISCO AT HOUSTON AND SAN DIEGO AT LOS AN-
GELES.

IN THE AMERICAN LEAGUE THIS EVENING, SEATTLE HOSTS CAL-
IFORNIA, TORONTO VISITS TEXAS AND NEW YORK HOSTS KANSAS
CITY.

SPORTSWATCH BY BOB KIMBALL
        AP-LA-04-09-86 1123 T
B195
    RO
    AP-TEMPERATURES
    HERE ARE THE LATEST WEATHER REPORTS FROM SOME KEY
CITIES AROUND THE NATION:

	F	C	
EASTERN UNITED STATES			
ATLANTA	56	13	WINDY
BOSTON	47	8	PARTLY CLOUDY
BUFFALO	38	3	SHOWERS
CARIBOU	35	2	CLOUDY
CHARLESTON, S.C.	66	19	FAIR
CINCINNATI	42	6	CLOUDY
CLEVELAND	37	3	SHOWERS
DETROIT	39	4	CLOUDY
MIAMI	82	28	FAIR
NEW YORK	54	12	CLOUDY
PHILADELPHIA	52	11	PARTLY CLOUDY
PITTSBURGH	37	3	SNOW
PORTLAND, ME.	46	8	FAIR
WASHINGTON	52	11	CLOUDY
CENTRAL UNITED STATES			
BISMARCK	56	13	FAIR
CHICAGO	48	9	PARTLY CLOUDY
DALLAS-FT. WORTH	62	17	CLOUDY
DENVER	50	10	FAIR
DES MOINES	52	11	FAIR
INDIANAPOLIS	46	8	WINDY

	F	C	
KANSAS CITY	56	13	FAIR
MPLS-ST. PAUL	50	10	FAIR
NASHVILLE	54	12	WINDY
NEW ORLEANS	69	21	FAIR
ST. LOUIS	55	13	FAIR

WESTERN UNITED STATES

	F	C	
ALBUQUERQUE	59	15	PARTLY CLOUDY
ANCHORAGE	10	−12	FAIR
LAS VEGAS	67	19	FAIR
LOS ANGELES	65	18	FAIR
PHOENIX	72	22	FAIR
SALT LAKE CITY	44	7	RAIN
SAN DIEGO	63	17	FAIR
SAN FRANCISCO	57	14	FAIR
SEATTLE	42	6	DRIZZLE

CANADA

	F	C	
MONTREAL	41	5	CLOUDY
TORONTO	39	4	WINDY

    AP-LA-04-09-86 1127 T

B196
    DA
    AP-RADIO-TV
    TURNER-MALONE
    (ATLANTA)—CABLE T-V BROADCASTER TED TURNER HAS
STARTED TALKS WITH THE HEAD OF THE NATION'S LARGEST CA-
BLE TELEVISION OPERATION.
    A SPOKESMAN FOR THE TURNER BROADCASTING SYSTEM SAYS
TURNER IS TALKING WITH JOHN MALONE—PRESIDENT OF THE
DENVER-BASED TELE-COMMUNICATIONS INCORPORATED—
ABOUT POSSIBLE JOINT VENTURES TO COMPETE MORE EFFEC-
TIVELY AGAINST THE MAJOR COMMERCIAL BROADCAST NET-
WORKS.
    THE SPOKESMAN SAYS TURNER AND MALONE TALKED FOR
THREE AND A-HALF HOURS YESTERDAY—AND THAT THEY
AGREED TO MEET AGAIN.
    THE SPOKESMAN SAYS MALONE CONFIRMED THAT HE WILL
JOIN THE BOARD OF DIRECTORS OF T-B-S IN JUNE.
        AP-LA-04-09-86 1129 T
B197
    UN

AP-(NORCAL BRIEFS)

(SAN FRANCISCO)—A JUBILANT MAYOR DIANNE FEINSTEIN SAYS THE BOLSHOI BALLET WILL PRESENT A WEEK OF PERFOR-MANCES IN SAN FRANCISCO IN AUGUST OF 1987.

FEINSTEIN SAID IT WILL GIVE PEOPLE A CHANCE TO SEE SOME OF THE BEST BALLET IN THE WORLD.

YESTERDAY'S ANNOUNCEMENT CAME AFTER CULTURAL EX-CHANGE PLEDGES MADE AT THE GENEVA SUMMIT IN NOVEMBER AND A TRIP BY FEINSTEIN TO THE SOVIET UNION IN DECEMBER.

THE BOLSHOI LAST CAME TO SAN FRANCISCO IN 1976.

(MARTINEZ)—A JURY HAS FOUND 26-YEAR-LD FREDDIE LEE TAYLOR GUILTY OF FIRST-DEGREE MURDER IN THE SLAYING OF AN 84-YEAR-OLD WOMAN.

THE SAME PANEL THAT CONVICTED TAYLOR YESTERDAY WILL BEGIN DECIDING APRIL 15TH IF HE SHOULD DIE IN THE GAS CHAMBER FOR KILLING CARMEN VASQUEZ IN HER RICHMOND HOME IN JANUARY 1985.

(SAN FRANCISCO)—MAYOR DIANNE FEINSTEIN SAYS SHE IS RE-SERVING FINAL JUDGMENT ON A PROPOSAL TO REQUIRE POSTING OF FOOD INGREDIENTS AT FAST-FOOD RESTAURANTS.

ALTHOUGH SHE LAUDED THE EFFORT, FEINSTEIN SAID SHE FIRST WANTS TO SEE THE FINAL LEGISLATION PROPOSED BY SU-PERVISOR WENDY NELDER.

THE MAYOR SAID THERE ARE A LOT OF ADDITIVES AND THINGS PUT IN FAST FOOD, AND PEOPLE HAVE THE RIGHT TO KNOW WHAT THEY ARE EATING.

AP-LA-04-09-86 1133 T

Index

Abbreviations, use of, 116
ABC (American Broadcasting Company), 15
ACLU (American Civil Liberties Union), 99
Actuality, in newscasts, 57, 74-75
Advances, types of, 66
Age, in broadcast journalism, 103
All Dimension Audience Research (radio), 17
American and English Encyclopedia of Law, 95
American Broadcasting Company (ABC), 15
American Civil Liberties Union (ACLU), 99
American Newspaper Publishers' Association (ANPA), 14
American Opinion, 96
Angles, news, 70
Associated Press (AP), 14, 30, 55, 56, 57, 59; audio service of, 57, 58; "splits," 57, wire copy, 131-53
Atlantic Monthly, 129
Attribution of news sources, 36-40
Audio roundup: AP, 58; UPI, 58-59
Audio tapes, free, received by radio stations, 69
Automatic release, 66

Backtiming, in five minute newscast, 107
Beeper telephone interview, 70-74

British Broadcasting Corporation (BBC), 21
Broadcast journalism: audience for, 46-47, 50, 51; and background knowledge, 12; colorful, 44-46; contractions used in, 43-44, 121; in conversational style, 19-22; coupling pins used in, 53-54, 106, 107; defined, 11, 12*n.*; and five minute newscast, 106-07; good taste in, 102-04; history of, 12-18; lead in, 49-53; and mini-documentary, 108-11; names of persons used in, 33-34, 104, 117, 118, 121; quotations used in, 41-43, 120-21; rewriting in, *see* Rewriting wire copy; sentence structure in, 19-22, 44, 47, 48-49; simplicity in, 46, 47, 129; sources of, *see* Sources of news; style guide for, 115-22; titles used in, 35-36, 117, 118; verb tenses used in, 30-32; and "warmup" of audience, 50, 51; writing techniques of, *see* Writing broadcast news; *see also* Radio; Television
Broadcasting Magazine, 92*n*
Broadcasting Yearbook, 76
Bulletin, news, 61, 105
Burger, Warren, 84

Cable television, 12*n*.
CBS (Columbia Broadcasting System), 13, 15, 17, 92
Circuit court, federal, 83